i

Ending The Migrant Crisis In Europe: Preventing Class Wars, Race Wars And The Destruction Of The EU

Bruce Masters

Copyright information

Thanks for Your Time

Hello, I just wanted to thank you in advance for your time.

I hope there is something positive, entertaining and useful in each of my books for everyone.

If you would like to reproduce any of my books for any reason, in any language or format, please feel free to do so for journalism, education or business purposes—if you can profit from my words, please do so, I will never request royalties.

If you enjoy this book, find it helpful, interesting or educational, please share a copy with a friend or tell others about these books and consider leaving a review or some feedback, which would be much appreciated.

Thanks again for your time. It is very nice to meet you.

Bruce

'The needs of the many outweigh the needs of the few.'
— Mr. Spock/the majority of EU citizens

Introduction

<u>Warning: This book contains opinions and tough love</u>

This work will assuredly achieve all of the following, if the recommendations herein are implemented:

- An end to skirmishes, deaths and violence on the EU's borders.
- An end to illegal immigration into Europe and the UK.
- The ascension of Romania and Bulgaria into the Schengen union.
- An innovative fast-track one-hour asylum process.
- A guaranteed migrant reduction of 99%.
- Cost effective and rapidly installed innovative border security.
- Greater responsibility and citizen involvement in governance throughout the Third World and Second World.
- The prevention of far-left violent revolutions, race wars and civil disorder in Europe.

The Opposite of Radicalism and Incitement

If I had spent these following chapters merely complaining about mass immigration, illegal immigrants, poor border security, non-integration of migrant communities, demographic change, native flight and balkanisation without offering any solutions to fix these many worrying problems, I would agree that this would be a radical book, a book that would cause incitement due to the reader being required to 'fill in the blanks' and decide for themselves what course of action needs to be taken in order to rectify these ever-worsening situations.

As it stands, however, for every problem raised within this book I have provided peaceful, reasonable and democratic solutions, suggesting the route forward is not a lurch towards radicalism.

This is not the time for fascism or Communism returning to Europe; no, instead we need to witness and experience an increase in real democracy. We need more referendums and greater cooperation between state representatives and taxpayers and we need our political representatives to be more accountable, more dutiful and patriotic and less self-serving, self-enriching and corrupt.

The radical thing would be to ignore this book. The radical thing would be continuing as though the mass unhappiness, angst and disquiet about all the many issues raised herein do not exist and everything is perfect and rosy and somehow, miraculously, tomorrow will be brighter than today without any changes being necessary and without the infusion of a great deal of political will.

Tone

My intent in writing and publishing this work is to decrease sectarian violence, decrease balkanisation and prevent civil war; as a result, my tone will likely seem abrupt, if not harsh, because my intent is not to make everyone happy. If it were, I would have become a stand-up comedian.

In this hour, the tone of this book is suitable, not perhaps attractive and palatable to every reader, yet suitable; suitable for the threats that face the lives of hundreds of millions of Europeans and thus the world, due to our maddening interconnectivity and interdependency.

Forgive my tone; forgive my inability to be politically correct; forgive my honesty and directness as these things will help you. Someone needs to be the opposite of everyone you prefer to listen to in order to create balance and ensure against fascism, I am happy to be that opposite number.

Any anger directed at me is misdirected. I did not create the migrant crisis. I did not force the EU to be so liberal and generous that every man and woman from the Second and Third World would naturally desire to relocate to Europe. I did not start the fire, I am merely the fireman.

If you can tolerate my tone and honesty until the end of this work, you will find yourself agreeing with every word written in this book, every word. However, if you abandon it now, or after but a few chapters, you will be doing yourself a grave disservice whilst condemning genuine refugees who are currently suffering to a predictable fate. You will soon come to realise that I desire to help genuine refugees and Middle Eastern/African/Asian nations infinitely more than every EU politician and bureaucrat combined. Read to the end, my friends.

Some will call this an anti-immigrant book, but it is the opposite because to suddenly absorb into Europe every non-European who desires to become an EU citizen (tens of millions each year) would only very temporarily benefit the immigrants in question before the entire system collapsed, disadvantaging and traumatising immigrants and guest workers as much as the shocked and confused natives. This book makes the case that the best place for man to be is in his own homeland and if there's a dictator or bully there making his life hell, he needs to fight back rather than allowing such evil to continue whilst he retires to Berlin or Paris. Gone must be the days of allowing problems to fester in non-EU nations, this festering is only possible due to the pressure release valve that is mass immigration and generous liberal refugee policies in places such as the EU.

Is the EU helping anybody? The homelands of immigrants are not being helped; the migrants choose to self-ghettoise and the natives in Europe feel forced to engage in white flight, so who are being helped other than big business, NGOs and corrupt politicians? This madness must stop for the sake of all people everywhere as each new migrant/refugee accepted is akin to catching droplets of rain from a leak in your roof. The EU is running out of buckets whilst the roof is starting to collapse. The roof (the migrants' homeland) needs to be patched and patched fast; the buckets need to be removed and only then will the leak stop....

Contents

The Proposed Initiatives

- Immigration-based tax system – 'Immigration Opt-in'.
- New (cost effective) border security measures, including a new solar-helium surveillance blimp/balloon fleet.
- Fast-track, sub-one-hour polygraph-centred asylum interviews (Poly-interviews).
- Citizen exchange program – CEP (one in, one out).
- The Resettlement Lottery.
- Billboard and poster campaigns in Africa, Asia and on the EU's borders—paid for by profits from fast-track interviews. (The EU must be able to profit from immigration, otherwise it will be deemed to be detrimental by the native man and woman and terminated altogether.)
- Increased international police and governmental cooperation in regards to identifying foreign terrorists, criminals and undesirable citizens before their entry into the EU, aided by increased use of biometrics and expanded databases.
- Increased use of advanced biometrics in order to track, monitor and confirm individual and national identity. Fingerprints, photographs and saliva samples will be provided prior to the fast-track, one-hour 'EU interview' being granted, a pre-condition for entry.
- Restructuring of welfare, housing and healthcare systems, things that have come to be taken advantage of and abused throughout Europe. No more welfare dependency for foreigners or natives; a sudden lurch away from apathy, malaise, irresponsibility and surrender and an insistence on duty, self-reliance, self-control, responsibility and strength (the welfare loan system).

Chapter One — Cognitive Dissonance

The multiple, almost endless excuses, justifications and arguments to accept any and all refugees, illegal immigrants and economic migrants is cast-iron proof of deep cognitive dissonance, quite simply because good behaviour requires absolutely no excuses. (Bad/self-harming behaviour requires endless excuses.)

These are just some of the most common excuses/justifications used to push the cause of mass immigration and open borders:

'It's the Christian thing to do.'

'There for the grace of God go I.'

'They have suffered!'

'They are *our* responsibility.'

'What about just taking women and children?'

'Think of the children!'

'If we don't let migrants and refugees into our country they will hate us.'

'We are rich enough to afford to care for them.'

'Borders are artificial.' One world, one human species, one big state to provide for everyone.

'In our distant past, our masters and elites were imperialistic, so we now deserve to have mass immigration and reverse colonisation inflicted upon us today.'

'We need more workers to do the menial tasks that we refuse to do.'

'European principles.'

'It won't destroy us, we can take it.'

'Love thy neighbour.'

'We are at fault, we need to learn to be tolerant; tolerance is good for us.'

'They would help us if we needed help.'

'We have always helped people in need.'

'What doesn't kill us makes us stronger.'

'Who will fund your pension in the future?'

'Charity begins abroad.'

'We need foreign nurses and doctors because we are living longer and have a larger population now due to mass immigration.'

'It will be enriching.' (Despite most migrants and refugees choosing not to integrate if they are given the choice.)

'Importing millions of low-skilled workers will improve the economy and make everyone richer!'

'We have refugee programmes in place; we should continue to help the world.'

'We are a multicultural nation.'

'If we don't open the borders it will damage our standing in the world. No one would respect us if we sought to control the size and makeup of our population.'

'If we don't put others first we will be called fascists.'

'Migrants are people too.'

'If we hadn't been imperialistic in the past there wouldn't be so many migrants and refugees. This is all our fault.'

'Our country belongs to everyone.'

'The UN wants us to share the load.'

'We still have some room left.'

'What would Jesus do?'

'Increasing taxation will fund mass immigration and our refugee programs, so there is no downside.'

'God wants us to open the borders.'

'We have had it too good for too long.'

'Mass immigration = reparations and "justice".'

'If we don't let them in they will become our enemies.'

'We have international commitments; we have to stay the course.'

'It is easier not to resist.'

'Our culture is closed-minded, backwards and imperfect. We need to be enriched by other enlightened cultures; we need to learn from other cultures.'

'What's the worst that could happen?'

'Foreign restaurants are great, which means we need more immigration so we can continue to have unbridled choice in regards to where we dine out.'

'We will always be the majority (despite migrant birth rates being double that of native birth rates) so there is no need to worry, we are only resettling "a few" foreigners.'

'We (our race/nation/religion) are not special so shouldn't be protected by borders, let them in.'

'Other countries are accepting immigrants and refugees, which means we should also. We don't want to be different or independent, do we?'

'We need to give some of our land to foreigners because they have "outgrown" their homelands, which are terribly overpopulated and devoid of resources or space (because it has all been consumed). It is our responsibility to share the international burden because it would be racist to advise people to have only one or two children instead of six or seven.'

'Borders are racist.'

'If we don't open the border, it will mean we are racist. It is better to pay higher taxes and build millions of new homes for migrants and consent to the undemocratic creation of multiculturalism and thousands of mini-Kosovos and mini-Donbases instead.'

***

When I help a blind man cross the road, no one will ask me why I helped him, and I will never feel the need to justify helping him either because, for me, doing such a thing is instinctual, natural and correct behaviour. However, if I choose to share the fruits of my labours with complete strangers from the other side of the planet who hate me and hate my culture, every sane person will ask why I am doing such a thing, considering how many disadvantaged and underprivileged natives there are all around me in my ancestral homeland, where my family have dwelt for untold thousands of years—the foundations of Stonehenge are 10,000 years old.

In my book *69 Excuses to Drink Alcohol and 1 Reason Not To*, I explore excuse-making and cognitive dissonance at length. That book is a good primer on the subject of engaging in self-harming, masochistic and incorrect behaviour and enabling such behaviour via the use of cognitive dissonance—offsetting (overcoming) your natural instincts via the inclusion of dozens of spurious excuses, which on their own can easily be ignored, yet collectively the multiple excuses form into a singular belief system.

So in terms of alcoholism, the drinker needs the 69 or more excuses to maintain his self-harming and family/community-harming behaviour, which culminates in him saying, 'I am an alcoholic.' What he is saying is he has formed enough excuses to no longer be swayed by his instinct not to drink or his instinct not to get drunk. 'I am an alcoholic,' translates to, 'I have formulated enough excuses to counter any argument against me not drinking. There are more excuses to drink than not to drink. I have "re-educated" (brainwashed) myself into being a cognitive dissonant vehicle for self-harm and masochism. I no longer make decisions based on logic, Occam's razor or natural instinct; rather, the many small, desperate and emotional excuses to drink I make, when combined into a chaotic and contradictory bundle of excuses, become my guiding light, my north star, my out-of-control and irresponsible constant.'

'I am an alcoholic.' 'I am pro-open borders.' These statements are the same; it is the same person saying these things, a person who knows they can say the opposite but who is making the conscious choice not to because the person who says, 'I am no longer an alcoholic,' and the person who says, 'I am pro borders,' is a responsible person, all will agree, which speaks to the motivation for many choosing to support mass immigration and open borders as these are irresponsible positions that will cause chaos, helping the minority to the detriment of the majority. This is why responsible people battle and overcome their addictions and resolve to increase their responsibilities and duties in order to create a life worth living.

Ask a European man who claims to be pro-open borders why he continues to choose to live in a European country with European people all around him rather than relocating to a country in Africa, for instance—is he a dreaded racist? He will have multiple excuses, multiple lies ready and waiting to be used, as he also will have for claiming to want open borders. He is only pro-open borders so long as someone else is footing the bill – against their will – because he is the thing he professes to hate, a fascist, due to being opposed to the majority having a vote or referendum on the subject of immigration, borders or refugees. All such individuals (those who believe in minority rule/those who fear referendums) are fascists and supremacists at heart, albeit fascists and supremacists in denial.

He will tell you, 'Having open borders is the right thing,' that it is benevolent, it will help the economy (somehow), that we can learn so much from 'them', that borders are fascist, that borders cause racism and mistrust in institutions. He will give you as many excuses and lies as the long-term alcoholic gives in order to maintain his self-destructive course of action. Open borders are only possible if we first remove the state, and most are not yet ready for this bold step.

Ask him why he is thousands of miles from home (if he is trying to facilitate mass immigration into Europe through EU borders) helping complete strangers whilst there still exists native suffering, native poverty, native drug dependency, native inequality, native homelessness, native chronic loneliness and depression, native domestic abuse, native corruption and native crime. He will have no answer for you, which is why you should ignore him as he seeks to create new problems for his country before he has first fixed the pre-existing problems, the hero of his people he ain't.

Chapter Two — Immigration 'Opt-In' Taxation System

If you want to pay higher taxes to fund more migrants, more refugees and more external charity endeavours, your country should allow you to pay more tax; the EU should allow you to pay more tax.

If you want to pay lower taxes because you don't want to fund any refugee or migrant cause or external charity endeavour of any kind (for instance, if you are extremely poor and in bad health and not a homeowner) your country should not force you to pay for these things and the EU should not force you to pay higher taxes to fund these things.

Once implemented, the IBTS (immigration-based tax system, also known as the Immigration Opt-in option) would ensure that <u>only those who desperately wished for open borders were expected to cover the costs of housing and caring for migrants and refugees.</u>

No vote or referendum would be required to implement such a dual system as those who wanted to pay for refugees or migrants in general would only be required to tick a box on a tax form in order to signal that they wished to 'put their money where their mouth is' by opting to pay higher taxes in order to help foreigners, whereas everyone else need not do a thing as not ticking the box would ensure an instant tax reduction and thus an opting out of paying to house, feed and protect non-EU citizens.

Opting in would increase your tax from, say, forty to fifty percent; however, this could rise far higher if few others chose to opt in.

Within a fortnight, the results would be in; a referendum would have, in effect, been held on immigration and the result should cause millions of economic migrants to look elsewhere for a new place to live because it is predictable that 99% of people would opt out of paying for non-EU citizens.

Voters/taxpayers could opt out at any time (after opting in), but when this happened, the individual could no longer proudly display the poster in their window, which would read, 'I chose to pay higher taxes.'

If you love immigrants you will pay for them.

If the liberal teachers who regularly strike and protest because they believe they are not paid enough want to pay more tax, they should be allowed to pay more tax if it means helping asylum seekers and unfortunate foreigners. Yet, it is unlikely that such individuals who are at the forefront of the pro-immigration "cause" would be happy if only pro-immigration advocates were expected to feed and house outsiders—because if they were happy to suffer, why would they continually strike and march?

It is easy to shout, 'Let them all in,' when someone else is paying the bill, but when you alone have to pay, the shout soon becomes a muted whisper.

The end result of this common-sense proposal would be as follows:

Where currently the parents of all the children in a classroom pay more or less the same amount of tax (this could be the UK or Germany or France, for instance) as the teacher and headmaster, who are both staunch socialists and pro-multiculturalism and anti-borders, after the small tweak to the tax system everything would change, including the world outlook of the teaching staff.

The parents of the five children whom the teacher classifies as refugees or asylum seekers likely don't work and thus don't pay tax, so no change there.

The parents of several children who were born in other nations who relocated for financial reasons (economic migrants) will now be paying far less tax because they will, understandably, not wish to pay to support refugees or asylum seekers or simply non-working foreign born persons because they are choosing the path of work and sacrifice, so they desire everyone else to do the same.

The parents of the poorest indigenous children will now be paying far less tax because they will not choose to pay tax for the express purpose of importing new job competitors and their children and cousins and uncles.

The only parent in the room who will be paying more tax than before is the teacher, who is married to the headmaster. Both choose to use their principles and conviction and "morality" to decide how much of the fruits of their hard labours should be sacrificed in the interests of benefitting complete strangers who would never choose to pay higher taxes, in any situation, at any time, for any reason.

As the teacher looks around the classroom, she notes that the indigenous children are smiling; there is more money in their household. She notes that the children of economic migrants are smiling also for the same reason; she notes the children of second-generation African and Caribbean immigrants are smiling because no one in that community will ever put foreigners before the needs of their African-European or Caribbean-European children who were born and bred in Europe. And, finally, the teacher notes that the only child in the classroom who is not smiling is her own child, who is one of the pupils.

The teacher asks herself why the other children are happy, celebratory, positive and exuberant when her own child seems dour, demotivated, insecure and unhappy. *Is it because we had to cancel our foreign holidays this year because we chose to do the right thing by opting in to fund refugee centres, translation costs, legal fees, housing, healthcare and education for every foreign-born man, woman and child in the world? Or is it because the children and parents in our street laugh at us relentlessly due to the placard we erected in the front garden that states, 'Proud to pay higher taxes because we love refugees'? Or is it because my child feels disinclined to study hard or work hard because she is facing a future of extremely high individual taxation because she will of course be expected to choose to opt in at the very earliest opportunity because foreigners cannot be expected to save themselves?*

What parents will soon be marching, demonstrating, shouting, threatening strikes and complaining? That's right, only the teachers because after the honeymoon period (of feeling virtuous due to sacrificing a bit of their wealth) is over, once the self-abnegation begins to sting too badly, it is predictable that those who chose to pay higher taxes (who hitherto had always complained that they were not paid enough, perhaps because union fees and foreign holidays are very expensive) would do anything and everything possible to subvert democracy and the will of the majority by once again forcing one and all to pay for refugee centres, for welfare for migrants (who don't know the language or culture and who don't wish to learn these things). Those who initially pay the higher tax rate will soon become fatigued and wearied due to solely bearing the burden that they insisted enter their nation and community.

They will shout and shriek, 'This is not fair. Even though it was only liberal middle-class socialist saviours like me who demanded mass immigration and open borders and the admission of a hundred million or more refugees, the indigenous working class should be forced to share the costs of immigration and globalism, even though these things in no way benefit them. Second-generation immigrants should want to pay higher taxes also; everyone should welcome the opportunity to engage in forced and very selective charity.'

Eventually (it wouldn't take long, we all know this is true), those who initially opted to fund migrants and refugees would soon change their position because paying higher taxes isn't such a great thing when it means you are disadvantaged personally in a myriad of ways whilst your neighbours, who are the same in every way apart from politics and philosophy, enjoy an ever greater standard of living. Hearing champagne bottles continually being opened in neighbouring properties as everyone suddenly found themselves paying 10% less tax would cause the staunchest open borders activist (who finds themselves choosing to pay 10% more in tax) to adjust their priorities and their outlook in order to remain sane and solvent.

If the working class and second-generation immigrants (for instance) joined the very narrow group of middle-class liberals in their mission to 'save the world, one foreign citizen at a time' (a nonsense ambition) those in unions and in teaching and politics and the liberal arts would more happily tolerate their standard of living being massively detrimented due to the sudden tax increase—why? Because such people are communistically minded, they are happy to pay more (to fund their pet projects) so long as everyone else is forced to pay an equivalent rate of tax, with such higher taxpayers insisting that it is democratic to be forced to pay taxes to help non-citizens during a time of mass unemployment and homelessness and home repossessions.

The end result of this proposal (which doubles as a vote on immigration, demographic change, identity and individual freedom) will be fewer than 0.1% of citizens in the long term (the most self-harming, self-hating and masochistic citizens) choosing to pay more tax in order to pay the large refugee/migrant bill.

Those nations who adopt this policy can be assured that migration to their nation and refugee applications will massively drop, quite likely in keeping with the percentage of those who choose to pay the 'immigrant tax' (a tax on personal conviction). If only 1% of a nation's children choose to fund migrants and refugees, one can naturally expect a 99% drop in asylum applications, border incursions, and illegal immigration as well as legal immigration. So the nation with the highest percentage of citizens who opt to pay more to fund non-citizens will become the recipient of the largest number of migrants and refugees, which is guaranteed to cause the upper tax rate to increase monthly, if not weekly, due to migrants now ignoring nations that choose not to pay the higher tax option.

If 10% of Germans consistently chose to opt in to pay 15% higher taxation in order to fund refugees and migrants in every imaginable way, Germany would suddenly become like a flame, like a beacon. She would attract every migrant and refugee on the planet because ten percent of Germany would be declaring, 'We have enough land, properties, food, resources and wealth to share. Come here everyone, we will save you and give you fantastic lives!'

Within three months, the Opt-in tax rate (tax addition) would predictably need to be increased to 20% due to 1/ many Germans choosing to opt out after a few months of deliberate financial self-harm caused by them opting in and 2/ migrants being attracted to the generous Germans without considering, 'What happens when the middle class becomes overly burdened by high taxes caused by mass immigration, multiculturalism and their attempt to adopt the world?'

Within twelve months, millions of migrants will have settled in Germany. The country is at breaking point; its public services are overly strained, classroom sizes have doubled and the additional Opt-in tax rate has now reached 30%, meaning a school teacher in Germany will likely be paying 80% tax a year after opting in, whereas a German taxi driver or labourer will only be paying circa 30% tax.

As those who opt in are forced to pay ever greater amounts of tax in order to fund their dream of a socialist paradise, the newly arrived migrants will make statements such as the one below, intended to show gratitude but also as an attempt to keep the guilt-ridden privileged middle class as their eternal allies:

'We thank Germany for housing us and protecting us. We love all Germans, but we especially love the 10% of Germans who are happy to pay double the amount of tax because they are great and loving and caring human beings and we know this 10% of taxpayers will always be there for us. Thank you.'

Pros and Cons of Opting In—in Brief

Those who choose to pay the additional five or ten percent tax will be automatically thanked loudly and very publicly, including being encouraged to place posters in their windows or placards in their gardens crying out to all of their neighbours the fact that they are the kind of person who is happy to pay more taxes in order to improve the lives of non-citizens.

Those who opt in can of course choose to remain anonymous if for some bizarre reason they don't want people to know that they are heroic, altruistic or masochistic (depending on your point of view).

Despite being able to hide from their neighbours, friends, family and colleagues the fact that a taxpayer has chosen to opt in, which will declare, 'I support mass immigration and I love refugees,' it is assumed that few to none will do so, which will cause a predictable series of events:

All of the individual's neighbours suddenly asking for loans or free money as they share their own hard luck stories, bad memories and collective pain in order to emotionally elicit funds from their "generous" neighbour.

Refugees visiting the individual's property and asking in person for additional help and assistance due to them making it abundantly clear that they will give as much as they can to help foreigners.

Fewer foreign holidays and fewer bottles of champagne for 'champagne socialists'.

***

A typical example of not opting in:

A taxpayer in Germany, Mr Klaus, chose not to opt in; he chose not to place his tick in the box on the paper form; he chose not to text the word 'Yes' to the EU; he chose not to visit his local tax office in order to state 'Yes' in person—because Mr Klaus chose to pay as little tax as possible, knowing that the more tax he volunteered to give to non-citizens the more new non-citizens would be attracted to him and his generosity. Seeking not to become bankrupt and miserable, Mr Klaus simply did nothing, he did not need to vote 'No' because the new tax system was centred around opting in; only those who insisted on sharing the fruits of their labours with foreigners had to text, email, fill in a form or visit their local tax office.

After a period of two weeks, the German government sends Mr Klaus a letter confirming that he hasn't 'opted in'. This achieves two things: It gives him another opportunity to opt in (because he may have forgotten to text/email/fill in the relevant tax form) and it will tell him how much surplus income he will have this year compared to the previous year, if his salary is more or less fixed.

The letter:

Dear Mr Klaus,

Because you have chosen not to opt in, this year you will be paying €4145 less in national taxes.

(He will book himself a holiday immediately or pay to repair his roof.)

If you wish to opt in to help migrant and refugee causes, you can do so at any time via text, postal form or by visiting your local tax office and the German Government will increase your taxes immediately in order to assist those causes, after which you will be sent a revised tax statement.

***

All taxpayers will be told how much they will save if they don't 'opt in'.

Automatically, every taxpayer is opted out; they will have to return a form (or text or email/phone or visit their tax office) in order to guarantee their participation in the voluntary 'pro-immigration and pro-refugee tax'.

EU politicians and bureaucrats (and the leaders of non-EU countries who wisely choose to adopt the proposal also) will be blameless in regards to the democratic change because they merely gave taxpayers a choice.

Why having a vote on the adoption of 'Opt-in' is undemocratic.

EU nations shouldn't hold a vote on implementing Opt-in taxation for one very important and obvious reason: Because millions of EU citizens do not pay tax in any form and millions more benefit from mass immigration—the asylum lawyer will of course vote yes to more immigration, as will the slum landlord, as will recent arrivals who have been granted citizenship, as will those who hate Europe and seek for it to be changed or destroyed.

This change only concerns taxpayers; this only concerns contributors, which is why a vote is unnecessary and undemocratic. In this rare instance, however, of course the majority of taxpayers will certainly vote in favour of the Opt-in system.

Any change to the tax system only concerns taxpayers. Simply requiring taxpayers to opt in is enough to ensure democracy and equality throughout the EU. Those Europeans who are depressed by, displaced by and disadvantaged by mass immigration, demographic change and native flight deserve to be able to choose whether or not they should continue to be forced to fund the things that cause them to be miserable, apathetic and despondent.

Chapter Three — Restructuring of Welfare, Housing and Healthcare Systems

As has been evidenced convincingly elsewhere within this work, the vast majority of migrants and refugees entering Europe choose to gravitate towards those nations with the most generous welfare/benefit systems. Those refugees who have made it to France, a great and free and generous nation, often choose to risk their lives by crossing the treacherous English Channel in small dinghies. This proves that they are not refugees but opportunists. They are not in danger in France; rather, they are willingly putting themselves in danger by risking drowning in order to make it to the UK mainland where they will scream, 'Asylum, asylum! Please give me a British passport and a house and money.'

This is a legacy of empire, with many economic migrants who pose as refugees (because they wish to be kept for life) wrongly believing that Britain still 'rules the waves'. These days, Britain is massively overpopulated and a shadow of her former imperialist self; however, other than being drawn to Britain's 'power', fake refugees come for welfare, for housing, for healthcare and it will all be free in perpetuity, why? Because of the struggles and sacrifices of the working class and unions in the past. A lot of marches, a lot of strikes, and a lot of hard work secured social benefits and welfare and state housing and education for the poor. These things were not benevolent gifts from the elites or middle class; no, these things took immense struggle and upheaval.

The obvious fact is if Britain stated tomorrow that all welfare payments, all social benefits and pensions and free healthcare and free stuff full stop were all going to end, no more money for anyone unless they worked hard (which seems logical and fair) there would no longer be economic migrants, criminals and opportunists posing as refugees crossing the Channel, endangering their own lives as well as the lives of French and British coastguards. As a result, the number of migrants present in France would drop massively overnight, reducing the burden on that already overburdened caring and compassionate country.

Imagine that Britain no longer gave away anything for free to her own citizens or foreigners, why would a single migrant and refugee choose to take the additional trip across the ocean rather than settling in Germany or Italy or Romania or Poland? Why would any of these individuals want to come to Britain if there was no free house for them, no free healthcare for them, no pension for them, no free welfare payments every week, no free food for them, no free furniture for them, no free utilities for them, no free gas, no free water, no free electricity for them, no free smartphone and phone contract for them, no free legal assistance for them, and no free translation services for them all paid for by the hardworking and overburdened British worker?

The easiest way to end the problem of fake refugees as well as mass immigration is to stop giving everything away for free. This is madness, we cannot afford this. Taxes should reduce every year as we socially and intellectually evolve and as we reduce corruption, overcome crime and create utopias throughout the world. Tax should never rise, yet that is what happens every year, not including the stealth taxes such as rising rents and stagnation of wages at a time of high inflation due to the missteps of our national representatives....

Instead of saying to the poor of the world, 'Come to France, everything is free here,' or, 'Come to Britain, everything is free here,' one should say, 'Come here if you have something to contribute. We are willing to protect you but only if you are willing to protect us in return and become loyal to our nation, to sever old allegiances, to know and love our language and culture before you reach our shores, only if you integrate rather than self-segregate and self-ghettoise, only if you agree to pay back every single penny or cent loaned to you via the 'Welfare Loan System'. If an alleged refugee arrives with nothing, it will perhaps cost €50,000 to pay for his integration, accommodation, new clothes and furniture, healthcare, dental care and food for the first twelve to twenty-four months. This sum must be paid back; the generosity part is that this is an interest-free loan.

Those migrants/refugees who do not like this concept can apply for asylum elsewhere; they can drain someone else's treasury. The current situation is disgraceful and the cause of widespread racism and abject hatred of refugees, which sounds bizarre but is a reality because the soft and liberal welfare and benefits systems of the West treat foreigners with kid gloves, not wishing to appear racist in any way, because that is career suicide in this politically correct age. Clearly the combination of softness, liberalism and political correctness is not solving any problems but rather is the cause of problems multiplying for everyone.

There have been multiple cases of fake refugees, criminals posing as refugees and terrorists posing as refugees, including, for instance the cases of Khairi Saadallah, Emad al-Swealmeen and many others also who were granted asylum by Britain only to commit serious and deadly terror attacks on British soil afterwards.

The first step to deterring them would be to declare, 'There is no money left, nothing is free here anymore. If we give you money, you will be paying it back when you begin working.' Those who consent to such a reasonable and sensible demand will be deemed by all citizens to be genuine, creating a better atmosphere for all, including the migrants themselves, due to racial tensions and racism reducing overnight.

What do natives everywhere always complain about? Migrants/refugees 'living on welfare'. If it is no longer possible for migrants or natives, then complaints will end and all can focus on their own lives, getting their own houses in order and collectively making their nations into strong and supporting vessels that will carry the people who dwell within into the next millennium.

The Welfare Loan System should also apply to an eighteen-year-old native who claims he can't find work or a fifty-year-old native who claims the same thing, not only to ensure equality between all citizens (native and non-native alike, native born and foreign born, indigenous and refugee alike), meaning that foreigners are being treated just the same as natives, no better, no worse, but also, insisting that jobseekers' benefit/unemployment welfare payments and state funding of rent must always be repaid as soon as possible will have numerous glorious benefits for all nations wise enough to enact these revolutionary changes.

A fourteen-year-old young woman in England or France or Germany today knows that it doesn't matter all that much if she falls pregnant because the state will give her free money, free nappies (diapers), free accommodation, free healthcare, free, free, free, free—yet after this proposed change, she will know that these things are no longer free but rather temporary loans. When the same fourteen-year-old realises that her parents and family will be expected to repay this loan until she becomes an adult when that responsibility shall transfer to her, she will tell her boyfriend, 'When we are adults with work, a roof over our heads and stability, we can have sex. Being irresponsible and out of control now will doom both of our futures. I am not willing to get into so much debt; I haven't even lived yet....'

The Welfare Loan System will:

• End malaise and apathy and smash the depression and pessimism within every native in receipt of these welfare loans due to them suddenly being motivated, for perhaps the first time in their lives, to rise. Where previously there was no pressure to swiftly find work in order to survive, now the longer they choose to stagnate and avoid duty and responsibility the greater the size of their loan becomes.

• End the practice of living beyond one's own means.

• Create a new self-sufficient trend everywhere and cottage industries and self-employment, due to many seeking to escape dependency upon the state eternally (because they soon get bored of paying back the loans given to them for healthcare, dental care, housing payments and free food), which will result in thousands of new micro farms everywhere and hundreds of thousands of new small businesses. Entirely new industries will spring up almost overnight as every man and every woman suddenly stands taller and prouder, now physically and psychologically stronger as obesity and depression and addiction become things of the past, as fast food and self-harm are rejected as all seek a more natural and healthy existence, as credit and debt disappear due to all learning the value of living within one's own means.

• Reduce crime everywhere due to the sudden huge surge in profound self-respect and self-determination achieved via no longer 'giving people free stuff'. The man who yesterday looked the other way when drugs were being sold outside his child's school because of the free house and free food and free healthcare and free bus travel the state gave him will suddenly, in an awesome manner, feel compelled to keep his community and streets clean of any and all crime and criminals, whom he will talk to, whom he will try to reach, but whom he will not allow to terrorise his community a moment longer. When the free money ends, the bribe to be servile ends, so do collective apathy and dereliction of duty. Men everywhere will rise as criminals everywhere hurriedly reform.

• Cause a new love of state, of community, of the system and culture and society to flourish because no one respects the man who gives you free money whenever you ask him to, but everyone respects the man who says, 'I will give you money after you have first completed a useful or worthwhile task.' It is not love to give a man free things because it creates dependency and weakness in his heart, he comes to hate himself and then you, but if you give him work, or, better still, if you do everything possible to encourage him to become self-employed or self-sufficient (more must be done in this area, much more) then he will not only love himself after working for his reward, he will love you also, for not patronising him and for treating him like an equal rather than a ward or a lesser individual.

I would strongly recommend it being a prerequisite to qualify for any welfare loan payments of any kind to be a sober non-smoker with good physical health.

If an individual wants me to give them a loan (what the envisioned welfare/benefit payments would amount to) wouldn't I be a fool for handing over a single penny if the applicant was smoking expensive cigarettes, drinking alcohol, which is in equal parts expensive and demotivating (alcohol is a proven depressant), and morbidly obese?

If two applicants asked me to provide them with a loan, one was a healthy living, fit and self-disciplined man who wasn't killing himself with cigarettes or alcohol or drugs or similar self-harming behaviours and the other was the complete opposite, whom would I offer the loan to if I had to choose between the two men?

The 'nice guy' in me would feel inclined to help the man who seemed more desperate, who was destroying himself via his numerous addictions and a toxic lifestyle, clearly depressed, clearly long before having chosen to give up. But that would penalise the other man who made his bed at 7:30 a.m. even when he was out of work, who then ran five miles and completed several sets of push-ups and sit-ups before having a cold shower. This other man, this Spartan, this useful citizen, this patriot would deserve my full attention and the loan, whereas the other man should be starved of funds until his unnecessary and harmful addictions and habits fell away from him as he became physically and psychologically fit and healthy, for perhaps the first time in his life—boot camp/military service without the need for these troubled souls to be sent away anywhere. It is far better to trust people (especially men) to improve themselves alone, gradually, in order to build in them the type of character that will attract the best type of friends to them, the type of character that will attract the best mates to them and the type of character that will attract the best employers to them.

Such a system cannot be implemented overnight. Warnings would have to be given far in advance of the change in order to ensure that those who smoke, drink, have terrible diets and lead depressingly sedentary, unnatural lives, primarily in front of the television or in pubs or sports stadiums, would be able to adapt to the new universally beneficial order with the least amount of trauma and shock caused to them.

The interesting benefit of requiring those you help to be fit and healthy and non-smoking, self-disciplined and self-motivating non-drug users and non-alcoholics is that the education system and the media would naturally come to champion this cause as there are no downsides; everyone wins. Only apathy, pessimism, cynicism, depression, obesity and liver disease and cancer die! Let these things die!

The irony of insisting that a citizen could only qualify for state assistance if he was in optimum fighting fit health is that the moment he found himself out of work and standing in the queue outside the government welfare office where he would apply for a temporary welfare loan he would look himself up and down as he felt fear inside due to being unemployed and embarrassment and shame due to having to beg the state for a loan. And then he would realise that only the 'old him' needed help from anyone because the fear he was now feeling was an echo from before when he had expensive smoking and drinking and drug habits, when he lived a vain and affected life where he "needed" to spend a fortune on clothes and jewellery and the latest expensive phone, becoming something strangely artificial and certainly not human in the traditional sense.

This citizen, now self-disciplined and exercising complete self-control, in amazing physical and psychological health, would smile before leaving the queue. He would find a pen from his pocket, he would find a piece of cardboard in a bin he walked past, and, whilst continuing to smile from ear to ear, he would write down his CV and abilities as he walked through his local town shouting in a friendly manner to others as he held his sign proudly before him, 'I do not want to burden the state by applying for welfare. My previous employment ended one hour ago, I am ready to continue working immediately. I will do any kind of work; I will be an asset to you.' Within one hour he would find himself again in employment. Within five years he would be a regional manager. Within fifteen years he would own his own business, employing hundreds, and he would have done it all himself!

Man wants to thrive; we need to let him thrive. Survival is not enough. The meaning of life is not for humans to merely survive by subsisting off the state.

Chapter Four — Romania and Bulgaria in Schengen

For many years these nations have desired ascendancy into the coveted Schengen union, which would raise the standard of living for all Romanians and Bulgarians due to fewer (if any) border checks or tolls or tariffs. (Schengen enables free movement within Europe, which would have huge beneficial ramifications for Romanian and Bulgarian businesses, resulting in higher revenue, which would result in higher tax contributions in these very recent additions to the EU family.)

Year after year these nations have followed every order and edict from their partner nations in the EU in order to qualify for admission into Schengen, yet there is always some excuse or other that seems to keep these former competitor nations 'out of the club'.

Sometimes corruption is cited as the reason why they cannot be admitted—despite corruption being rife within the EU and Western Europe also.

Sometimes police brutality and a lack of diversity are cited as justifications for continuing to keep these nations out in the cold.

Yet more recently, the objections have been wholly centred on the issue of mass immigration owing to Turkey being located to the south of these nations, which is the bridge to Asia and Africa.

Through no fault of their own, these nations, which are trying to separate themselves from their communistic past and links with Russia, are being penalised due to African and Asian conflicts causing millions of non-EU citizens to migrate towards Berlin, Paris, Vienna and London—0.1% choose to stay in Bulgaria and Romania because they are among the least liberal EU states and because welfare in Western Europe is extremely generous.

These countries are damned if they do and damned if they don't. They can't win.

If these nations are liberal and relaxed in regards to non-EU citizens transiting through their territories en route to 'the West' (most non-EU arrivals only use Balkan nations as a bridge to Germany, France and the UK), nations such as the Netherlands and Austria respond viscerally by banning Romania and Bulgaria from joining the coveted Schengen Agreement, as has been the case this week (the first week of December, 2022); whereas, if these nations take a hard line on the border and 'get physical', they receive exactly the same response. Romania and Bulgaria cannot win. If they let migrants in they are punished; if they are too forceful with illegal immigrants they are punished and scolded. This situation is untenable and ridiculous. Something needs to change, immediately.

Bulgaria and Romania desire Schengen membership due to perks such as it becoming cheaper and easier to trade with the remainder of the EU bloc.

If, however, both nations attempt to prevent every non-EU citizen from entering the EU illegally, the same nations (as well as the EU as a whole) scold the most recent additions to the EU family by criticising violence at the border, encouraging the protectors of south-easterly EU borders to be as peaceful and gentle as possible with the people who are attempting to 'break into' Europe, an impossibility when faced with belligerency.

These new EU nations can't win.

Too relaxed = no Schengen.

Not relaxed enough = no Schengen.

And these nations can forget about the euro, as what liberal German or Italian wants his currency shared with nations who use 'fascist tactics' in the interests of protecting all Europeans? (Bulgaria was due to adopt the euro in 2024, this has now been postponed.)

Romania and Bulgaria feel frustrated and trapped. Already these nations are lurching more towards the right and nationalism, becoming ever more hostile to the foreign citizens (primarily young men) who they have been informed by the EU are the cause of their nations and economies being 'held back', which causes the very real perception of inequality within the EU family. Cries of racism from citizens of both nations are spread across social media and frustration is growing.

If these nations are not permitted to enjoy the same freedoms and privileges as their EU neighbours, it will not be long until anti-EU feeling spreads, with there already being talk of a RomExit and a BulgExit. If either change occurs (or if both nations choose the path of independence, like the UK) the conflict on the EU border will no longer be taking place in the Balkans as freedom from the EU would permit Balkan nations to use every means possible to end the flow of migration from the south.

Leaving the EU would end illegal immigration in the new non-EU nations whilst creating new EU border conflicts elsewhere—Greece, Italy, Hungary, Austria, Spain.

If those being frozen out of Schengen don't very soon receive the support and respect they clearly deserve for doing an incredibly difficult job, such nations will choose a new path, a new direction—because what the EU currently demands is an impossibility. These brave men and women are on the one hand being ordered to keep every illegal immigrant out of Europe and on the other hand they are told that they need to keep out the most belligerent, the most criminal and most aggressive international trespassers in a peaceful, loving and dignified way. Surely this is a contradiction? This leaves everyone on every side feeling rather confused and fed up.

Romania has expressed a great deal of interest this week in joining with Moldova—the bridge to Ukraine and Russia.

Few desire this in Moldova, other than the large Romanian contingent (understandably), yet in a year, maybe two, advancing Moldova into the EU (she would become an automatic EU member if annexed by Romania) may become the desire of the majority in that nation, suffering terribly as a result of the conflict between her neighbours to the north and to the east.

If this happens, it will create ripples.

Bulgaria (a long-time close ally of Russia, with shared cultural, ethnic and language roots) will be more inclined to embrace 'old alliances' if she cannot receive fair treatment within the EU, which more and more of the disaffected EU states, such as Hungary, Romania and Bulgaria (the UK was once on this list), see as benefiting some nations and demographics more than it benefits others.

With her recent fifty-five-year history of communism (only thirty years have passed since then) and due to Russia being intrinsic in her liberation from hundreds of years of Ottoman rule (1878), many young and unhappy Bulgarians see rejoining the Eastern Bloc as a preference to remaining in the EU as a junior member who is unendingly chastised and raked over the coals when all they are trying to do is protect the European Union.

Would Romania have floated the idea of the annexation with Moldova if she had been granted the coveted Schengen membership in 2021 along with the euro and massive new investment in infrastructure, especially in underprivileged rural areas? Perhaps not, perhaps not.

And looking to Bulgaria, this is the only EU nation where pro-Russian protests and marches have taken place in the capital, such as protests against sending weapons to Ukraine, where a recent (March 2023) NATO survey revealed more than 50% of Bulgarians 'wouldn't help a NATO ally if they were attacked'.

In both nations the situation is tense, due to EU inequality, EU supremacy, the conflict in Ukraine and the impossible-to-adhere-to guidelines that every police officer and border guard is expected (by Brussels) to follow.

If an unidentified young man, wearing a balaclava, throws a rock from Turkey at the face of a Bulgarian police officer, solider or border guard, the EU expects them to retreat and hide (because EU bureaucrats project their own psyche upon their vassals and protectors, this is unwise) rather than stand and fight—the way every man would if his house was being invaded, if his vulnerable and beloved family slept peacefully inside.

The EU wants to have their cake but eat it also, this is impossible. If the EU refuses to station non-Bulgarian and non-Romanian EU border guards on her frontiers, replacing the Romanians and Bulgarians because the native officers and guards are 'too defensive', how can she complain when local men do anything and everything necessary in order to defend their homes?

I am sure the EU is pondering the creation of a dedicated EU border force (similar to UN peacekeepers), which could help to accelerate Romania and Bulgaria into Schengen; yet the border skirmishes could be the cause of Bulgaria crashing out of the EU long before EU taxpayers have been convinced by their superiors in Brussels to foot the bill for the thousands of new guards and thousands of miles of new border fences and walls....

Chapter Five — Taxes, Prison Sentences and Deterrents

Currently the deterrents in place are not good enough, not strong enough to prevent potentially millions of illegal immigrants from entering the European Union (and thus nations such as the UK) each year.

The obvious and knee-jerk solution would be tougher sentences for the very serious crimes of people smuggling, drug smuggling and gun running; yet there is a downside to this solution—European taxpayers being forced to pay to keep non-citizens in prison for years or decades. There is no money to pay for this; there is no desire to pay for this.

Instead, it is far better to disincentivise illegal immigration and smuggling of every variety via the use of other means, such as the Opt-in tax system and the reassigning of border security to the armed forces, who will ensure a near 100% reduction in incursions across the EU's southern border.

Whenever one proposes longer sentences, they rarely think about the taxpayers who will be funding these longer sentences. One should always think about taxpayers first, which means implementing many or all of the suggestions offered herein.

Whilst the other recommendations mentioned within this work will indeed reduce instances of people trafficking/sex trafficking in general, there will still be those who insist on trying at all costs to break the EU's rules, why? Because the reward (working in the grey economy in Europe, being able to claim asylum, getting access to free healthcare and welfare in the West) far outweighs the risk of potentially being apprehended.

With this in mind, I suggest shifting the focus away from extended prison sentences (which will financially cripple Europeans) and focusing solely on profiting from the criminals, criminal gangs and smugglers who are undermining the EU in every regard.

If the apprehended individual, who will be considered an invader or trespasser (when a men enters your home without permission, what is he?), possesses assets/property/savings, these things shall be confiscated by the EU immediately, even if doing so requires communication with his homeland to ensure adequate compensation is paid to the EU in order to cover the costs of the translators that were necessary after his/her arrest and the meals and healthcare and lawyers that were all required following their arrest and the accommodation and security personnel who were also needed following their arrest and detention, as well as the cost of the judge or magistrate and a whole host of other combined costs, which in every instance runs into tens of thousands of euros at a minimum.

Those who pay criminal gangs to smuggle them into Europe routinely pay upwards of €6000, this has been widely reported. What this evidences is these individuals, both those who pay to be smuggled as well as those who carry out the smuggling activity, are not poor, not by a long stretch. What homeless German, Brit or Frenchman could muster €1000, let alone six thousand?

Step 1. If illegal immigrants are found in a vehicle and it is established that the driver is complicit in the criminal conspiracy to break a whole raft of EU rules and laws by importing illegal immigrants of absolutely unknown origin, the vehicle shall become the instant property of the EU, it will be sold at auction within seventy-two hours.

Step 2. Any money, valuables, jewellery, mobile phones, laptop computers, electronics in general shall instantly become the property of the EU. The money will be spent on the food and healthcare that the EU generously gives to the criminal group whilst all other seized assets shall be sold at auction within seventy-two hours.

Step 3. All individuals shall be held in detention, without a trial or access to legal counsel, until such a time as the following conditions have been met:

- They each agree to voluntarily leave the EU and never return.

- They each provide detailed information about the criminal networks that operate the people-smuggling, drug-smuggling as well as sex-trafficking operations in the European Union—names, telephone numbers, identities.

- They each give a detailed list of their assets, property and savings and/or a list of the properties and assets and savings of their family members and friends, as well as contact information for all of these individuals—due to the EU incurring extremely high costs every day the uninvited criminal trespassers remain in EU custody.

Step 4. Once the illegal immigrant has compensated the EU fully, they are (at their own expense/the expense of their friends and relatives) instantly deported to their country of origin or the last safe nation they were present within (for instance, Turkey).

Detained illegals would know well in advance that this protocol would be in place. They would know that (if caught) they would be forced to contact their parents in Iraq or their friend in Somalia or their cousin in Egypt in order to have funds wired to the EU in order to pay for the costs of their care and detention and, latterly, to cover the cost of their deportation also.

As a result of this foreknowledge, illegal immigration and smuggling would massively reduce because, suddenly, in order to be free, in order to return to their old lives rather than injecting themselves into another's land without permission, imposing themselves upon EU and UK citizens, they would have to near bankrupt their friends and relatives back at home, who would never think about smuggling themselves through international borders or climbing over border fences. This will act as a huge deterrent due to those back home feeling obligated to help the individual yet angered by having to help them also. Not angered at the EU, no, the EU has done nothing wrong; rather, they will be angered at the criminal who is draining the resources of the EU as the costs of policing, border protection, detention centres, and food and healthcare for non-citizen trespassers skyrocket.

The likelihood of those illegal immigrants who routinely pay thousands of euros to criminal gangs to aid their journey to Europe and the UK not being able to pay for their return journey and to cover the EU's cost of apprehending them, processing them and keeping them in detention for a few weeks are slim to none. These are not poor people; poor people do not have thousands of euros to give to smugglers.

Once the payments have been made, the illegal immigrant should be free to go, yet the cost of release/deportation should exceed what the EU has spent. For instance, if the EU spends €39,000 to apprehend, process, detain, feed and care for a single illegal immigrant for a period of ten days, the cost to the illegal immigrant's next of kin, family members and friends shall be €45,000—the profit would enable the EU to pay for more border fences and more security in general.

The 39,000 euro figure will rise each week, the illegal immigrants would know of this fact before entering Europe illegally, which will cause two things to happen: 1/ They will insist on the most basic form of detention, without perks, in order to keep costs to a minimum because they will be paying for their stay and 2/ It will cause their relatives and friends to reimburse the EU as soon as physically possible, obtaining second mortgages if necessary, selling cars and land if necessary, selling jewellery and televisions if necessary.

In regards to the smugglers themselves, they should (and will) be expected to pay at least double what the individual illegal immigrants are forced to pay, not only compensating the EU fully but also paying such a large fine to discourage any other man or woman anywhere in the world from ever thinking about people smuggling, sex trafficking or drug smuggling or gun running into Europe ever again, totally ending illegal immigration and restoring law and order along all of Europe's borders.

The driver who knowingly smuggles people into Europe will have been paid €20,000. The fifteen or twenty people he illegally brings into Europe have all paid his boss €5000 each—there is a lot of money in organised crime.

The money paid to the low-level smuggler is now forfeit—this belongs to the EU.

The smuggler is held in detention until he identifies his boss. His boss will now be arrested and all of his assets, property, and savings seized and transferred to the EU. Cooperation with third-party nations would be easily facilitated, especially with nations such as Turkey. The Turks are, of course, angered that millions of non-Turks are using their proud nation as little more than a 'staging ground' to enter Europe; how demotivated and depressing this is for Turks, how insulting this is also. Turkey will assist in rooting out criminal gangs, as will all other nations that seek to have friendly relations and good trade with the very influential EU.

Once the first illegal immigrant goes through this process, once they are deported from the EU within less than one week, €30,000 poorer (their family and friends and neighbours as well as themselves €30,000 poorer), illegal immigration will end.

Once the first smuggler goes through this process, €80,000 poorer, the criminal gang they are a part of will splinter and fragment, paranoia and hysteria overcoming them, not knowing what, if anything, the smuggler told the EU authorities about the criminal gang. Within no time at all, such individuals will realise it is far better to start a reputable business or work for an employer than run the risk of losing everything to the EU and their tenacious 'collection department', which soon develops an international reach and everything will be recovered, plus interest.

A typical phone call from a Berlin illegal immigrant detention centre in 2025:

'Hello, Father? Yes, it's me. I have arrived in Berlin, but there is a problem; the EU have captured me. They have taken my valuables and money and my mobile phone, they are looking through all of my contacts on the phone now, soon they will know all about the criminal organisation I used to get to Berlin.... Yes, I know you warned me about this … yes, I am sorry for causing you this stress, but I wanted to come to the EU.... Yes, I know I will have to pay for my stay in Berlin now … yes, I know I will have to pay for my deportation, I knew all of this before I came, I took the risk.

'So, Father, can I please ask you for a favour because I don't want to live in this detention centre? I want to come home, I made a mistake … but be quick with transferring the money because the total increases by the day! Go to my room, there is some money in the green book on the bookcase; take that and sell my computer and furniture and my motorbike from the garage … and I swear I will pay you back for paying for the rest … this is just a loan, I promise. When I come home, I will work harder than ever and I will never leave again … I said I promise … I will never try to enter the EU again, I have learnt my lesson.'

In regards to those who claim they cannot afford to pay for the costs of their stay with the EU and to recompense the EU (and thus working-class and middle-class EU taxpayers) in every regard, they shall remain in detention until pro-immigrant/pro-open border NGOs or those who put the interests of non-EU citizens before the interests of EU citizens valiantly come to their aid by paying to the EU the requisite sum in order to deport the individual in question out of the European Union.

Chapter Six — Poly-Interviews

Ukraine recently inspired this advice.

Recently (2023) there were (at least) 340 places of worship throughout Ukraine that were searched by the Ukrainian police/military in the interests of (it was stated) stamping out fifth-columnism.

Hundreds of nuns and priests were questioned as part of the ongoing investigation (into Russian interference/influence) as well as fifty of them being connected to polygraph machines (lie detectors), it was widely reported.

If these machines are reliable enough to be connected to priests and nuns, why can't they also be used on EU borders? This would A/accelerate Romania's and Bulgaria's entry into Schengen and B/massively reduce the numbers of migrants who are camped on the Union's borders, waiting for an opportunity to 'break into Europe'.

Poly-interviews would act as a deterrent because only genuine refugees would be able to complete the interview process successfully, whereas everyone else would be banned from entry into the EU in perpetuity.

Background

There exists so much propaganda (on both sides, between those who want open borders and no identity and those who prefer nation states and identity) that it is impossible for the layman to know who is an economic migrant, a persecuted refugee, a Jihadi, an escaped psychiatric patient or a people smuggler, it's a minefield.

Those who wish to defend nation states, rules and order claim that every man on the other side of the fence is 'bad for Europe'.

Those who wish to have a world with open borders, no rules and disorder claim that every man on the other side of the fence is 'good for Europe'.

Both sides are wrong because things are not always so black and white, which is why we need to discover the truth of the situation based on facts, rather than based on the opinion of people who have bias one way or the other. I have visited the borders in question, I have seen the migrant camps; I have been exposed to the apathy, hate, frustration, fear, hope and abject human despair in such places.

There is a mixture of people in such places, many of whom are vulnerable, many of whom have serious mental health complaints, which are only worsened by their prolonged limbo on the exterior of the EU's borders. The human mind can only tolerate so much—those who suffer from mental illnesses (schizophrenia, for instance) are best served remaining in their homeland, where they speak the language and are intimately familiar with the culture and cultural norms).

On the other side of the EU border fence are both good, great and bad, victim and bully, sex trafficker and humble labourer—because humanity is on the other side of that fence. No two migrants are alike, no two refugees are alike. (If you don't prejudge members of your own tribe and think them 'all the same' you shouldn't prejudge members of another tribe and think them 'all the same' either.)

If we say, 'They are all bad people,' without getting to know them, it means that we are bad people for prejudging them.

If we say, 'They are all good and innocent people,' without getting to know them, it means that we are naïve or deliberately deceiving ourselves, merely hoping that those who try to illegally enter our land and who intermittently throw rocks at the heads of EU policemen and border guards will be peaceful, passive and well-behaved once granted entry to the EU. Who wants their protectors to be attacked with rocks?

We must say, if we wish to be honest, that there are countless thousands of people on the other side of the fence who will seriously damage the EU and hurt EU citizens and economies (as well as peace and social order and community cohesiveness) if their pressure, violence and intimidation campaign (which has raged on and off for years, this new violence at the border is nothing new) succeeds in keeping Bulgaria and Romania out of Schengen—because the events following such a setback for those nations would cause shockwaves between Bucharest, Sofia and Ankara (with the entire region becoming fractious and tense).

Might these two nations choose to leave the EU if their work on the border (their protection of the EU) fails to result in Schengen membership? Stranger things have happened—after all, Romania and Bulgaria were sworn enemies of the West less than thirty-five years ago and close allies of the USSR with both being long-time Communist republics.

So, yes, there is a possibility that a Schengen snub, in tandem with recessions and the fear-inducing conflict in Ukraine, may create an atmosphere of defiance, an atmosphere of independence—and an atmosphere of rage; much like in 1987 when ethnic Turks in Bulgaria were forced, at gunpoint, to change their names/culture in order to be harmonised, in order to 'become Bulgarians'. Hundreds of thousands fled to Turkey rather than change.

Poly-interviews in Practice

What this new process and approach replaces is years and years of appeals and legal intervention and hearings at huge public expense. The true cost of mass immigration into Europe is astronomical, so far EU taxpayers have paid billions to help non-EU citizens, but with the help of this book, we can prevent that figure accruing extra digits because before too long the bill could easily transform into trillions.

The first thing you will notice is the new system does not require a lot of manpower or personnel, due to the system primarily being automated.

An example:

A repurposed van or minibus is driven to the border.

It reverses to a border wall where there exists a door.

The door is opened and the border guards of that nation communicate to the hundreds or thousands of people gathered there that they can apply for asylum if they enter the EU Poly-interview vehicle (there are reportedly four million migrants living in Turkey who desire to enter the EU immediately, who claim to be refugees).

Inside the vehicle there are cameras and sensors, computer screens, microphones and speakers—everything necessary to conduct a rapid (sub thirty-minute) asylum interview; this number can and should be reduced in order to further reduce costs and to process the huge backlog of applications, the interview would eventually be reduced to circa ten minutes only.

A voice says in multiple languages that the individual needs to place their hands on the fingerprint scanner; the voice tells them to pose for photos and tells them to use the swabs in the drawer in front of them to take a sample of their DNA for testing. The same voice will communicate that this information will be cross-referenced with every criminal and terrorist database in Africa and the Middle East, which will cause many migrants to choose to abandon their interview at once (those who are trying to hide their past or are intent on hurting Europe or her people).

Whatever the result of the automated interview and asylum hearing, the fee paid by the aspiring immigrant for the service will remain with the EU. There will be no refunds for any reason—due to those present within Turkey being able to visit the German/French/Italian/Romanian/Polish Embassies in Ankara to apply for asylum in the regular, internationally recognised fashion. The fast-track application is a perk and the refitting of vans and buses and the inclusion of advanced technology and polygraphs and AI is not cheap; these costs will be recouped, and recouped fast, Poly-interviews should be profitable within twelve months.

Within minutes of the interview process beginning, the interviewee's fingerprints are automatically checked by dedicated computer programs to ascertain whether or not the individual is a threat to the EU. If they are, for instance, wanted by the Egyptian government for rape or murder, the interviewee will be arrested and sent home.

Using a mix of touchscreen and voice recognition solutions, the interviewee will be able to make their case for entry into the EU. They will have the same chance as everyone else to enter the Union, but if consistent lies and deceptions are detected during the interview the result will be their claim for resettlement/asylum/entry into the EU being rejected. (Every device within the van or room is a part of a greater polygraph system— pupil dilation, heart rate, perspiration, anger, fear; these things and more are continuously monitored by advanced AI.)

I would strongly advise against permitting any sort of appeals process due to the cost, complexity and the fact that it would bring this most perfect system based on truth and facts into disrepute as any appeals that would follow would solely be based on emotive factors, which would precipitate an ugly competition between non-EU citizens who would each be claiming that they have suffered more than their compatriots standing to their left and right.

It is possible for interviewees to say 'the wrong thing' once, twice, even thrice during the Poly-interview before being banned for life from the EU (this warning is given prior to the interview, no genuine refugee would fear such a caveat) because the purpose is not to ensure 100% failure but to give everyone an opportunity to realise their dream of relocating to the European Union.

Those who answer every question successfully, who do not lie during the interview and who make it abundantly clear that they will follow every EU rule and law and integrate into the family of EU nations will discover that there is a second door in the van, which opens up on the EU side of the border. Whereas those who fail the interview, who have been exposed as liars, smugglers, terrorists, racists, misogynists or criminals in general, will be notified that they are banned for life from living in any EU nation, banned for life from receiving welfare or healthcare in any EU nation and, further, are banned for life from purchasing food goods of any kind or renting accommodation of any kind in any EU nation.

Who Won't Be Paying for These Tests?

The last thing the European Union should do is force EU citizens who have done absolutely nothing wrong (unless you call trusting the EU to protect them doing something wrong) to pay for the polygraph tests or for translators or the legal representatives and all the rest of it. Those days are long over because no one wants a return of fascism; no one wants race wars; no one wants Europe to explode in a fire of sectarianism or taxpayer fury.

Neither will the operation 'run at cost' because the EU needs to start serving her people rather than serving other people, which means the new EU entrance tests (the fast-track paid option) will be profitable for the EU and thus EU citizens, profitable in a myriad of ways, including:

The entrance tests may cost only €300 each, yet the EU will charge €600.

The EU offers a product (EU citizenship), which is why many illegal immigrants routinely pay upwards of €6000 in order to be relocated from the Middle East or central Africa to Berlin, Paris or Rome.

It Is Profitable in Other Ways Also

It is immediately assumed that the fast-track entrance procedure (one hour to become an EU citizen, versus five years for instance, what the wait may currently be for those who live for extended periods on the border who repeatedly attempt incursions into Europe whilst their asylum claims are being processed) will result in circa 95% fewer people at the border, due to the new tests ignoring emotion, tears and stories as they instead rely alone on facts, facts, facts.

If the EU wishes to exist beyond 2030, it is advisable to only induct those non-citizens who are the most honest, most hardworking and most deserving. These new tests ensure just that, the longevity of the EU—until all citizens are offered referendums (like Brexit), of course.

Even the most left-wing journalists and 'bleeding heart liberals' will soon shift their stance on supposed refugees/asylum seekers when they observe most refusing to submit to the Poly-interview process, as they ask themselves, 'What are they trying to hide if they're genuine refugees and believe in EU principles and socialist values and mean no harm to Europe?'

Regarding the Cost of Poly-interviews

If the migrant/refugee is unable to afford the application cost (again, European taxpayers should not pay for this service) who will cover the cost? Liberal Westerners, the clergy, pro-open borders NGOs and 'white saviours'.

The EU should encourage all conscientious citizens who value non-citizens more than citizens and who have money to burn to make donations to charity initiatives in regards to facilitating hundreds or thousands of these fast-track sub-one-hour tests.

Where Will the Profits Go?

The EU has a rare opportunity in this moment. Via the use of this initiative, the EU will be able to solve multiple complex issues at once: Pay for new border security, keep harmful individuals out of Europe, remove the untold thousands camped out just on the other side of the border whilst concurrently helping to reduce the tax burden for every EU taxpayer.

The EU will not be using the money she saves from this new enforcement measure (in tandem with the other advisory measures mentioned herein) on foreign aid or translation services, for instance. If I choose to relocate to China I will learn Chinese in advance and I would never expect China to give me money or 'free things' unless I was a patriotic Chinese citizen present within China....

This money will go back into EU economies in the interests of reducing taxation as much as possible for all Europeans as high taxes guarantee xenophobia and discord when the EU houses millions of refugees and migrants. Ever lower taxation is the guarantor of the longevity of the EU experiment and perhaps its only hope of survival—continued mass immigration will have the opposite effect.

Conclusion

Those who pass the tests will be granted asylum by the EU and those EU countries that have voted (there must be a vote, surely?) at a time of high unemployment, poverty and inflation and war to absorb new citizens who are unable to support themselves or help the EU will become the new homelands of these new EU citizens.

The interviewees who insist on choosing what specific town in what specific country they be resettled in are not refugees but nomadic window-shoppers. The EU desires to help people in need, fine, but if those in need refuse to be saved and protected by Slovakia, Poland or Romania they cannot be called refugees or asylum seekers, with the moniker of 'selective refugee' or 'economic refugee' being far more apt and accurate.

Despite all the many positives achieved by the implementation of such a scheme, there will still be those who will ask, 'Should we ban the fast-track one-hour EU citizenship truth-and-fact-based entrance test because demanding that people tell the truth and be connected to a lie detector is "fascist"?'

The answer to such a question is no.

At least not so long as all EU citizens are not permitted to have a Brexit-style referendum on being members of the EU, a situation that everyone must acknowledge appears very fascistic.

The precedent has already been set (Brexit); the continental European Union will do everything possible to prevent further independence referendums taking place.

So to criticise the use of a lie detector for being fascist yet not to criticise current EU practices seems both bizarre and hypocritical and unusual in solving the situation amicably for all parties.

EU citizens did not cause the refugee crisis; EU citizens should not be punished for the refugee crisis and EU citizens, the vast majority of them, agree with every single word written in this book. If you disagree, hold a vote on immigration or refugees or simply introduce the change to the tax system known as Opt-in.

It is also very unfair for European Union states to misrepresent their true nature by meeting prospective citizens in a friendly, caring and loving manner and purporting to care about their emotional state and their backstory because the unemployed EU worker knows that, in truth, in reality, his state, be it Italy, France, Germany or Britain (when she was still an EU member before choosing the tougher yet more rewarding path towards freedom and independence) will care little if he is too apathetic, sad, or lacking in motivation in that week, which caused him to remain unemployed because the unemployed EU citizen, which is what every refugee and illegal immigrant entering Europe automatically becomes, very quickly learns that no excuses are tolerated and constant proof of job searches is required, mandatory attendance of training courses in exchange for welfare is required.

The indigenous EU citizens, especially in the working class, will feel second class when expected to adhere to rules and behavioural norms whilst new citizens are able to avoid them wholly.

So, this is as much a warning to non-EU citizens as it is an exposé of EU hypocrisy and affirmative action/masochism.

Chapter Seven — The Two-Billion-Euro Border Fence and Helium/Solar Blimps

It has recently been suggested that the minimum cost of securing the EU's southern border would amount to €2,000,000,000, but, of course, these huge projects always cost double or triple the original estimates. But let's keep the low two billion figure for now, which Romania and Bulgaria cannot afford to pay and which the EU have already stated they refuse to pay, claiming it is the responsibility of every nation to ensure their borders are fully secured.

During the Cold War, there was no movement on the Turkish border, no man entered or left because the border at that time was guarded by the military, on both sides.

It is only now that Bulgaria and Turkey are allies (in NATO) and that Bulgaria is a member of the EU that we see huge waves of migration permeating through the now sieve-like southern border. Something is not working; something must change immediately because those who break into the EU illegally give every good and honest migrant and refugee a bad name. They cause fear and paranoia and xenophobia to increase every year, month, day and hour.

The solution is obvious, use the nation's military to secure the nation's borders—and the cost of border security would be covered by the pre-existing military/defence budget.

When you see a sign that says, 'Danger, military testing ground,' or, 'Danger, minefield ahead,' you instinctively start walking backwards in order to protect yourself and it does not matter whether or not there are walls or fences between you and the mines or between you and the military base because the mere existence of these things in your path ensures that you will turn around and go home.

Once the EU begins guarding her borders with her strongest defenders (her armed forces) books such as this will no longer be needed as the military will ensure that the defences of the EU become impenetrable. Why would any EU citizen desire anything less?

It is easily possible to transfer thousands of acres of border lands to the military with the land migrants once passed through now being occupied by the military who use said land for training, testing of weaponry and for guarding the interior of their nation—a physical internal buffer. When the border guards or police say, 'Please climb down off that border wall,' migrants laugh and then throw rocks, but when the military says, 'Get off that wall,' the response will always be the same, compliance. The waves of migration will stop the moment the EU stops projecting weakness and charity and tolerance.

'A Bulgarian police officer shot and killed a migrant in the Bulgarian countryside' sounds bad, yet 'A Bulgarian soldier on a Bulgarian military installation opened fire when an unknown group of individuals penetrated the security of the military installation' sounds reasonable and proportional—the world would know that to enter Bulgaria illegally (only illegally) would mean trespassing onto a Bulgarian military installation/training ground.… Illegal incursions would drop massively overnight.

Border Blimps

The armed forces could easily install and operate the proposed fleet of helium surveillance balloons, which would be solar powered and tethered to concrete pads 100 metres from the border and would include night vision and heat vision cameras, movement sensors, communication-jamming equipment and powerful spotlights. (People/drug/gun smugglers rely on cell phones to coordinate their incursions into Europe; these blimps would jam such communication whilst tracking every human on the other side of the border twenty-four hours per day.)

These balloons/blimps are just one option to increase the physical effectiveness and cost effectiveness of border security; one blimp could easily prevent 1,000 intrusions per annum and there could be 1,000 blimps located across the entire southern borders of the EU. These devices, primarily maintenance-free, would serve the dual purpose of protecting individual states from terrorism, from military invasion, whilst ensuring that every movement, every action is recorded, documented and tracked. It would not be possible for abuses of any kind to take place on the border, by any side.

The proposed fleet of 1,000 blimps, however, would likely not be needed as the first dozen would have the psychological impact of deterring all but the most reckless migrants from attempting to illegally make their way into Europe in order to work in the grey economy in some fashion or wrongly claim they are refugees, which benefits no one, other than themselves.

A dozen blimps plus the military on the border (as in the Cold War) and 'Opt-in taxation' throughout Europe would be more than sufficient to end the migrant crisis once and for all.

Two billion (at least) saved.

New purpose for armed forces.

New technology for combatting crime, terrorism and fifth-columnism (Poly-interviews, surveillance blimps, etc.).

What is the downside? Higher prices for the middle class and elites in restaurants because the owner is finally forced to employ natives to cook, clean and wash dishes because he no longer has access to an unlimited flow of illegal immigrant cash-in-hand workers. Cry me a river.

Chapter Eight — The Right to Buy Food

There are millions of illegal (undocumented) aliens living throughout the European Union and the UK—there are one or two in the US also, I hear.

Many are victimised by those in their own communities, working for pennies in kitchens or brothels. The situation is bleak and depressing; no one wants this situation to continue, surely? But how can we end this situation without knocking on every door in Europe in order to find and then deport every illegal immigrant, which many would term becoming hyper-fascistic? (This is what would eventually be required if every suggestion herein is ignored, in order to avoid the total collapse of the system.)

The introduction of the policy 'The Right to Buy Food' would solve the problem immediately because a man (illegally in your country, who does not pay tax or contribute and who will not defend your nation in any way in times of war) can get a cash-in-hand job in a restaurant or a car wash or building site and he can sleep on the floor of an overcrowded migrant house and can drive his (legal) friend's car from A to B, but unless he has an official identity card/document and is playing by the rules, he will not have earned 'The Right to Buy Food'.

This means the next time the illegal immigrant in question, who climbed over an EU border wall or paid people smugglers €6,000 to get him to Berlin, attempts to purchase groceries with cash using money he made from the grey economy, he will be told, 'You do not have permission to shop in this supermarket because you cannot prove who you are.' (Imagine in 1942, at the height of rationing, if German fifth-columnists present in the UK were allowed to purchase British goods in British shops just because they had cash money. It could easily have caused the collapse of the British war effort….)

Simply requiring all citizens to show proof of identity when they purchase groceries, fuel (gas/petrol/diesel) or attend a doctor's surgery or hospital will completely end illegal immigration today.

This is not something I or anybody wants to happen, yet it may be the thing that needs to happen to discourage more illegal immigration, to reduce racism and xenophobia and to wrestle back control from criminal groups and illegals who exist outside the rules and order of the EU and EU nation states.

What citizen would be outraged when asked to prove they were a citizen when purchasing diesel or cucumbers or cat food? Only those who don't want illegal immigration, smuggling, disorder and wide-spread crime and the grey economy to end—and such people can either choose to be good citizens by carrying the requisite ID on their person (the way they currently carry their driving licence with them) or they can protest against this measure, in which case they will be fined, with the money they pay in fines to the EU being spent solely on the deportation of illegal immigrants. Eventually, sanity and sense will reign once again.

Checking the identity documents of every citizen in Europe—if you don't have the courage to do this you need to step down. There are many with the strength and stomach for such an undertaking. What honest and law-abiding and honourable man would be angered by the authorities who protect and serve him asking to see his identity documents (documents that only exist for verification purposes)? The only ones who would complain would be spies, anarchists, criminals or illegally present individuals (illegal civilian occupiers), ICOs.

You would never be able to use any state hospital in Europe or the United Kingdom if you failed to pass the simple entrance tests.

Chapter Nine — ZeroP Policy

The ZeroP policy = Zero Percent refugee admission, Zero Percent illegal immigration admission, Zero Percent economic migrant admission.

If a single nation had a zero percent refugee and migrant policy (in effect, closed borders) it would suggest that the one nation in question was somehow in the wrong, due to all other nations 'sharing the burden' of housing and protecting refugees and economic migrants from less wealthy and more overpopulated lands.

However, when every nation has a ZeroP policy (there exists a philosophical wall around the territory of every nation) no nation can be accused of racism, supremacy, elitism or bias. What is created is equality; what is created is self-reliance and self-determination; what is created is an insistence on living within one's own means, careful and considered procreation; what is created is a new future, a future where there are no refugees because if there is no way out, one must stand and fight against apathy, pessimism, weakness, depression, fear and bullies. One must be more responsible; one must insist on demilitarisation; one must hold politicians accountable and ensure against conflicts with their neighbours.

A zero percent refugee/migrant policy would mean there would never again be a refugee or illegal immigrant or economic migrant created anywhere for any reason. This is the brave and beautiful future all EU/US/Western citizens crave in their hearts, a return to natural instinct and humanity, which means fighting for survival rather than being the Third World's 'always there' insurance policy.

If Americans had chosen the refugee path, the USA would be owned by Britain today, but they stood and sacrificed and fought and died so their sons could enjoy liberty, rather than fleeing to South America, for instance.

The nation that drags her feet the most in regards to the implementation of ZeroP will be forever known as the greatest enemy of refugees and, more so, the greatest ever enabler of injustice, depression, oppression and apathy in other nations.

The first nations who embrace ZeroP will be saying, 'It is because we love refugees that we are turning them away. Their children and grandchildren will thank us for what we have done because we are not only motivated by a desire to prevent ghettoisation and balkanisation and racial and religious conflicts form taking place in our homeland but also by a desire to liberate the hearts and minds of non-citizens everywhere, who we want to become independent, proud, strong and free in their own homelands, rather than choosing the 'live for today' option of emigration.'

Sex traffickers, terrorists, economic threats, smugglers, criminals, fake refugees, escaped criminals and escaped psychiatric patients—they are all stopped by ZeroP.

I want every country to have a ZeroP policy, which will create equality, self-determination, an end to corruption and a beautiful new and free future for every man and woman who today is destined to become a refugee or economic migrant due to the mistakes of politicians and broken immigration systems designed only to benefit big business.

The majority of people value identity and freedom first and foremost; however, what identity exists in the town where you were born and where your ancestors were born when, almost overnight, suddenly, ninety languages are spoken in addition to the native Italian or Spanish or English?

I have seen the migrant camps in Turkey, I have witnessed the thousands of babies there, all born well after their parents left their homelands, all conceived and birthed after their parents had entered Turkey. In addition to these many babies, small children are also observable there, hundreds of thousands of small children, all conceived and birthed during times of civil war and tribalistic conflicts in the homelands of their parents—would these babies and small children exist if ZeroP existed? No. Why? Because the parents would know that if they produced children they would have to care for them in perpetuity, rather than being able to rely on Turkey or the EU or the USA to care for them, feed them, house them, provide healthcare services and education to them.

An absence of ZeroP creates recklessness and a spirit of dependency, whereas ZeroP creates individual responsibility and independence. Is producing children during a time when you cannot feed or protect yourself a wise thing to do? No, no, it is not, and it is not the responsibility of other nations and taxpayers from other nations to pay the cost of the mistakes of reckless non-citizens from many countries away.

Those impacted the most by ZeroP will suddenly find that they are forced to stand up to bullies and dictators. The refugee/migrant currently has a choice to leave, so guess what; he leaves, but when this choice is taken from him, he has no alternative but to work harder, struggle harder, fight harder and win his freedom, his independence, and in so doing will achieve what the Russians achieved after their revolution, what the French achieved after their revolution, what the Americans achieved after their revolution— international respect and a country worth living in, worth fighting for, worth dying for.

'But we need immigrants and low-skilled workers,' I hear someone in the EU or the UK say, who must have a vested interest one way or another in keeping borders open and thus causing multiple crimes to forever continue.

To this I reply, 'Would the EU die without immigrants?' No, the "need" for immigrant labour is a need to stagnate wages in order for big business to make greater profits. The "need" for immigrants is to pay native workers less. The "need" for immigrants is to render unions null, void and obsolete. The "need" for immigrants is to hurriedly introduce as many consumers in one place at one time, which benefits those who own properties and build properties, those who work in the civil service and those who work in the immigration/refugee sector. It was claimed that the first West Indian migrants were needed by Britain (to primarily drive buses and perform similar working-class roles) because Britons refused to do such work. Rubbish. The natives only desired fair pay, which is why mass immigration began, because employers always prefer the desperate and grateful foreign worker over natives because they will complain less and be happy to work for less.

Chapter Ten — The Twenty-One Types of Pro-Mass Immigration and Pro-Demographic Change Advocates/Activists

(And the One Type of Anti-Mass Immigration and Anti-Demographic Change Advocate)

Many are understandably confused as to why the demographics of their nations are suddenly changing as we begin this new millennium.

Some believe there must exist some sort of nefarious conspiracy or global plan that is responsible for this change. This is not the case.

I approached the writing of this chapter in the same way I approach every task in life, via the use of Occam's razor: 'The simplest explanation is most often the correct explanation.'

With this in mind, I was able to identify the twenty-one separate groups of individuals below whose separate and unique motivations disprove all conspiracy theories in regards to mass immigration, native flight and demographic change whilst also helping to expose numerous bad practices, bad actors and disingenuous 'pro-immigration' activists.

This chapter will provide some insight and will aid those listed below also in terms of this chapter acting as a mirror because perhaps this would be a good time for all of these groups (the twenty-one types) to focus their attention and care solely on their home. It is my hope that everyone everywhere adopts the logical approach of 'charity begins at home', which will create universal equality—rather than the current situation of, 'Help others first; put yourself and your family last.'

If every family looked after themselves properly, why would one family ever require the help of other families or of the state?

A sudden demographic shift is taking place worldwide, affecting multiple continents and dozens of nations.

These migrant waves are directly caused by globalism, multi-nationalism, welfare/benefits, greed, want, entitlement, envy, free movement and liberalism. But beyond these factors, achieving such feats as deliberately engineering complete multiculturalism, causing mass native flight (referred to in some nations as white flight) and precipitating the importation of hundreds of foreign cultures, hundreds of foreign languages and millions of people required the support and assistance of certain unique types of native citizens, twenty-one types to be exact. In no discernable order, they are:

1. The Middle-Class Racist-Narcissist-Supremacist
2. The Business Owner
3. The User-Consumer
4. The Corrupt Politician
5. The Compassionate Narcissist
6. The People Pleaser (Those who just can't say, 'No.')
7. The Victim of Stockholm Syndrome
8. The Privileged Malcontent
9. The Far-Left Activist
10. The Missionary/European Saviour
11. The Bitter Inciter
12. The Privileged Masochist
13. The Victim of Peer Pressure
14. The Fashion Victim/Trend Follower
15. The Fetishist/Submissive
16. The 'Fake Nazi', who seeks anarchy and destruction
17. The Modern Feminist
18. The Profiteer
19. The Elites—in sheep's clothing
20. The Guilt/Pleasure/Reward-Driven Christian Zealot
21. The Tinpot Dictator, the Tyrant, the Oppressor of Humanity

The Middle-Class Racist-Narcissist-Supremacist

'I vote for the Green Party; I have a lot of disposable income; I was very well educated; my political and philosophical views are the correct views because I carefully consider everything I do because I am superior to most people in my own nation, most of whom are terrible racist knuckle-draggers. So if I am superior to my own people I am certainly superior to non-citizens, which suggests they can't ever be expected to create a good country for themselves because they are not me. They are not blessed by liberalism, good placement within the class system (fluke of birth) and the dozens of luxury foreign holidays I have enjoyed over the years that have enriched and expanded my mind, causing to increase my supremacy and feelings of self-worth and high status. I will continue encouraging mass immigration—just not to my local area, which I insist remains exactly the same way.'

The Business Owner

'Sir, the local men cannot afford to feed themselves or their families. If you don't pay them a fair wage their suffering will only get worse.'

'But what happens if I stop paying them completely? Is that what they would prefer?'

'But you cannot do that, sir, because we have a union and we pay the union a lot of money to protect us. We will become so loud and cause so much trouble, sir, that you will happily give the men a ten percent wage increase, which is all they are asking for.'

'I cannot do something? You are replaceable, all of you are replaceable. You may have the union, but I play golf with the local MP and mayor, I attended Oxford University with the home secretary and I donate a hell of a lot of money to certain political parties, so I am not worried whatsoever. The only question that remains in my mind is should I turn this factory into luxury flats for liberals and coffee shop junkies who will gentrify the hell out of this area and send your jobs to China or should I "encourage" a politician to make yet another very passionate pro-immigration speech as the pretext and justification for importing your willing replacements—who will work for half the money, agree to live in crowded conditions, who will never join your union and who will cause a massive wave of native flight whilst I grow richer and fatter?'

The User-Consumer

User—uses everyone.

Consumer—consumes everything, even when doing so detriments others.

Some people are pro-mass immigration for ethical reasons due to the strength of their "convictions" or for religious reasons and others for philosophical or political reasons—yet the user only thinks of himself and is only driven by a desire to preserve himself for as long as possible for no discernable reason.

The user thinks to himself, *I want to live in great comfort forever, if possible, which means we need to create new members of the working class to serve me and keep me for as long as I demand to be served and kept…. What do you mean local birth rates are plummeting because the natives are now more cautious and are using contraception? How dare they! No problem, simply swing open the gates and allow a few million far poorer and far more desperate people to enter our community; that way there will be new and grateful young people to tend to my every need, to work in the kitchens of restaurants, to wash my car, to cut my grass, to build my home extension, to care for me in a retirement home and to do everything else I request them to do. So what the indigenous poor are miserable? I only care about me, me, me.*

The Corrupt Politician

The man who seeks to use immigration for creating political capital, as part of a social "progressive" agenda, who (in reality) knows the only ones who benefit from sudden waves of mass immigration will be big business, due to wage stagnation.

This "pro-immigrant" individual is anything but. He is happy for foreigners to become ghettoised and live in overcrowded dwellings and districts and he is only happy for the foreigners' homelands to become replicated all around him because he financially benefits from immigration. However, you will not find him on the ground floor but rather in the guarded penthouse apartment, his ivory tower.

The Compassionate Narcissist

This individual favours momentarily uplifting the disenfranchised despite the evidence suggesting that such an action will endanger the entire system or society in the future—feeding wild animals your leftover food because you feel "pity" for them, without a thought for the repercussions of your actions on the ecosystem or about the dependency you are creating, due to only thinking about how the act of giving makes you feel, how helping improves your own happiness.

It's like saving a child from a burning building whilst recording the incident on your smartphone.

It's about wanting that situation to continue, so in the case of feeding stray animals (who the helper believes need to be helped—by them alone), if they (the animals) come to reject the offer of assistance or if they suddenly gain weight and seem healthier, the "giver" will be displeased. In the same way, those who assist migrants in their quest to leave the Third World for the First would be displeased if the migrants chose instead to work harder in their homelands to improve their situation rather than giving compassionate narcissists exactly what they want: the pleasure they receive from maintaining their position of superiority over the migrants and the pleasure they receive from "helping".

He wants the pain of animals and humans he has compassion for to continue, just as he wishes for himself to eternally continue, unable to imagine that he could ever die, due to narcissism being for life, not just for Christmas.

He would instantly become angered if the stray dogs he feeds suddenly appeared better fed one day, if he could no longer see their ribs due to another man beginning to feed them also. He wished to be their saviour, their only saviour, yet he would not wish for them to be instantly healed or improved; rather, he would wish for these strays to forever remain in their same state, skinny, dishevelled and begging for his scraps. In order for him to derive pleasure from remaining in the same mode (maintaining the same degree of compassion, enjoying being compassionate) the animal or man or whatever he chose to favour would have to remain forever the same, unchanged.

The fellow who feeds small birds in his garden tells himself he is a good person who loves animals due to having compassion for the birds, proven by the fact that he erects a bird feeder, filling it with a multitude of seeds and nuts. However, when a squirrel or large bird approaches, he viciously scares it away. And if the small birds he claims to have compassion for, whom he seemingly loves and favours, manage to spill the entire contents of his bird feeder upon the ground, instantly gaining access to two weeks' worth of food, the man will not be happy, he will likely curse at the small birds due to them refusing to abide by his strict rules.

Sometimes it seems that someone cares when they don't care. Sometimes a person can seem loving, generous, benevolent and kind when, in reality, they are a monster.

The People Pleaser (Those who just can't say, 'No.')
(Irresponsible and insecure people with out-of-control emotions)

'Mummy, can I have another biscuit, please?'
'Daddy, can I stay up until midnight because it's New Year?'
'I have had this pet cat for one week; can I change it for a pet dog now, please?'
'Can I eat some chocolate and sweets before dinner?'
'Can I build a tree house at the top of the tallest tree in the garden?'
'Can I have some fireworks so I can have fun with my friends in the park?'
'Can I drive your car please, Mummy, just in the car park?'
'Can I stay at home today, Mummy? I don't want to go to school today.'
'Daddy, can I have a beer?'

We all know people who are unable to say, 'No.' This type of individual (sadly for them) will feel forced by every request for help to empty their pockets, their purses and eventually open their doors also in order to make everyone happy so that they will feel loved, accepted and a good person or a good parent.

Giving your child what he wants just because denying him (protecting him) makes you seem like the bad guy is a guaranteed formula for disaster. If generous and giving people are not very cautious and measured, they will soon find themselves becoming masochistic missionaries or being imprisoned and having their children taken into state care because when we instinctively answer pleas for help with 'Yes!' we doom ourselves to an existence of being used whilst concurrently dooming he who asked for help to a life of unrewarding irresponsibility.

Mummy was irresponsible because she permitted her son to stay out late at a young age with much older boys; a few months later, he has impregnated a young girl, been arrested for graffiti and has started drinking and smoking, all before the age of fourteen. This is not uncommon in the 'Yes, yes, yes' modern West, where no one, it seems, has the strength of will to simply say, 'NO!'

Those who can't say no should stay away from borders and conflicts because they will always choose to surrender to the will of others and embrace meekness, passiveness and irresponsibility because they believe they will be liked or even loved if they behave this way; whereas, in truth, yes men and yes women are universally held in disdain and are respected by no one. 'My mother? No, you don't need to worry about her, I control her; she gives me anything I want, she is a glorified slave. I can never do any wrong, which is why I am not rushing to get a job or work hard because she will be there forever to save me, to give me what I want, and she will never say no to me....'

The Victim of Stockholm Syndrome

'Let me in … let me in … LET ME IN!' Kane from the movie *Poltergeist II* insisted to the shocked homeowner, Steven Freeling, who felt pressured enough to consider allowing that movie's bad guy into his home, which would certainly have endangered the welfare of his entire family. Steve stood paralyzed as his mind sought to make sense of the situation: *Someone is claiming to be a nice and good and peaceful person and all they are asking is to be allowed to enter my home. Why wouldn't I, why shouldn't I just acquiesce to their will?*

Those who have been victims of extreme bullying, coercion, psychological manipulation and narcissist partners or relatives in the past will find it hard not to open their door when certain very pushy individuals, insistent on entering their home, simply ask, 'Please open the door. I am a good person; I have suffered. Let me in.'

The gaslighting and extreme pressure will seem familiar to the one-time victim of Stockholm syndrome, which is why they will lower their guard as a means to defend themselves individually from those who refuse to enter their nation the right way, the legal way, the non-aggressive and non-bullying way.

Is there suffering and sadness and innocence on the border? Yes, but are there visible aggression, bombast, bullying and threats also? Of course, the world has witnessed such things again and again, which causes he/she who suffers from Stockholm syndrome or has a predisposition to being used by narcissists or bullies to overnight become the defender of every migrant, just as the hostage often defends the hostage taker many years after their harrowing ordeal has ended, even advocating for them publicly and calling for their release from prison.

This type of pro-immigrant and pro-open border advocate is more common than many might think, and they are a danger to themselves as much as anyone else and certainly should not be considered thought leaders due to their motivations being born out of fear and a corrupted (traumatised) psychology.

The Privileged Malcontent
(Who wants to hurt Daddy)

Revenge, pure and simple.

If a teenage boy from Somalia, for instance, really wanted to hurt his middle-class Somali father's feelings, make him scared and anxious and make him feel absolutely powerless and defeated, all he would need to do is listen to his father and perhaps make a few notes.

He will quickly discern what exactly drives his father and what demotivates him also. He may learn that he fears Christians (perhaps he is Muslim) and he fears too many men from the neighbouring country moving to his country because the other country is in the middle of a bloody civil war.

The teenage boy, approaching adulthood, was raised in a privileged and middle-class manner, he has a great standard of living thanks to his father; he feels so special, in fact, and superior that it vexes him whenever his father tells him 'no' or whenever his father ignores him or belittles him or says, 'When you grow up you can have this or that….'

When this boy becomes the age of a man, he still thinks and acts like a boy as he begins encouraging mass immigration in order to spite his father, in order to make him feel as powerless and afraid as he felt growing up. The boy doesn't think about himself being hurt by importing an unlimited number of resource competitors because he is monotropistically lost in his cause: Hurting Daddy whilst pretending to be a hero.

The Far-Left Activist

'All are equal, so we should all suffer equally.' This activist wants to create an equilibrium between his nation and the poorest and most disordered nations, and he knows the quickest way to achieve this equality is to import millions of people from those countries and encourage them not to change a thing about themselves, which will shock and surprise them but they will gladly agree to export the culture they thought they were leaving behind because to them it is familiar and thus comforting and assuages feelings of guilt and regret at leaving, surviving and prospering. The migrant/refugee feels guilt due to leaving his homeland, which is ironic because the far-left activist only encouraged him to abandon his homeland due to himself feeling guilty due to being born into privilege—the multiplication of guilt, guilt causing guilt, unhappiness causing greater unhappiness.

The far-left activist praises diversity and change, he calls it progress, and relishes the fact that conservatives and nationalists, libertarians and the self-motivating are scared about social change and higher taxes because they are all his competitors (think the Lord Mandelson immigration comment, 'We wanted to rub their noses in diversity.') He not only wishes to make them miserable, he wishes to control them completely via a one-world 'people's government'.

This zealot's mission is to defeat the spirit of his people and defile the character of his homeland, which was the end result of thousands of years of struggle, evolution and supreme effort.

The Missionary/European Saviour

'If we don't feed the Third World we (rather than they) will be responsible for their fate. My superior ethics and morality mean that I must help those who wouldn't help me and who have absolutely no interest in adopting my religion or praying to my god. I don't care if they hate me and only want to be friends because I give them money, clothes, housing and protection because I am superior and forgiving and tolerant. But I will not tolerate foreigners having to fix their problems themselves because, as a wise narcissist-masochist, it is my responsibility to get their house in order for them, isn't it?'

The Bitter Inciter

This type (primarily wives and daughters) use immigration as a means of stirring or stimulating native men to change, evolve or 'rise to the challenge'. They deliberately employ racially charged incitement with the expectation of causing jealousy, insecurity, embarrassment, shame and anger:

'You now have to compete not only against all native men (whose abilities and tactics, strengths and weakness and virtues are known to you) but also the men from the rest of the world (who are a mystery to you, which is why you are suddenly very anxious and thus angry because people fear and hate what they don't understand).

'So what are you going to do? Be forced by me to feed, clothe and house the men from foreign nations whom I bring before you, be my powerless cuckold, or are you going to get your house in order and work harder to impress me? I have more choice now, which means you have less power, which means I have more freedom. Now you know how women feel; now you know what fear and powerlessness feel like.'

The Privileged Masochist

This activist prefers to smuggle the least educated, oldest and most disabled non-EU citizens into the EU because he has privileges and advantages and is guilt-ridden and ashamed. He believes that causing detriment to his homeland and the EU will somehow atone for imagined sins—this is the same man who allows his baby to go hungry because a slightly smaller (less well-fed) baby was crying somewhere else, far away.

This activist is dangerous because his intent is to cause pain and suffering to Europe and Europeans under the guise of being a saviour. If you save a non-working or disabled man from drowning, you become responsible for feeding him and tending to his every need.

This activist knows that those on the other sides of the walls and fences have absolutely no way of supporting themselves in Europe; he knows they will need to be 'nannied' in a myriad of ways. *But that's okay,* thinks the activist, *because we will simply increase taxes.*

These individuals are engaged in a long-term war against themselves. They practise self-hatred and self-abnegation habitually, thinking first about the woes of others most unlike themselves and only second about their wives and children, which is why most of these activists are single because they are terribly unhappy people who derive only a shallow sense of satisfaction after increasing pressure on the state, on local communities and on the European Union by sponsoring mass immigration and balkanisation throughout Europe.

'I saved the day!' is not something they can ever say because their actions have only caused to increase racism and Euroscepticism, disenfranchise the working class and enlarge non-conformist migrant enclaves throughout Europe, setting the scene for obvious future tribal tensions and conflicts—research the history of balkanisation and of Yugoslavia for a probable future vision of European nations unless the EU increases its power. To 'rein in' so many rivals who clearly don't wish to live together the EU may even have to suspend democracy by 2040 or 2045 because the alternative might just be the collapse of the European Union (unless advisory books such as this are taken seriously). People will only take so much for so long until they push back.

The Victim of Peer Pressure

'Hey Tom, why haven't you donated to the refugee cause yet? You're not a racist are you?'

Conformity offers protection, which is why the Third Reich was so successful in terms of the majority of the populace 'getting on board' with even the most heinous acts against mankind (against minorities) because even though every individual knew what was taking place was wrong, the peer pressure exerted by every individual guaranteed conformity—because 'if you are not with us, you are against us!'

Peer pressure in relation to mass immigration or refugees is immense and is a total 'black and white' affair. There is no grey; there is no exception; there is no third position tolerated; you are either progressive or a Nazi. This is sad; this is wrong; this is terribly tribal with echoes of 'One People, One Nation, One Leader' (with the people being EU voters, the nation being continental Europe and the leader being progressive liberal ideology and groupthink).

The Fashion Victim/Trend Follower
(Jumping on the bandwagon)

Driven by insecurity or a lack of an individual identity, many will queue up for as long as possible in order to purchase the latest social justice badge, wristband, or other such "proof" of virtue, intellect and empathy—signalling one's goodness and follower status.

Those who wish to be popular will always attach themselves to the latest cause or movement, be it abortion rights, animal rights, refugee rights, the right of every human on Earth to move to your town and every other social struggle and cause. It is only ever 5% of those attached to these causes, or less, who are actively involved, with the other 95% merely feigning enthusiasm as they seek attention and acceptance and seek to avoid being 'left out'.

The Fetishist/Submissive

(There is understandably some crossover here with the category of masochist.)

There are those in our societies who fetishise ethnic minorities; a famous example is Asian pornography, a disturbing type of erotic "entertainment" primarily consumed by Western European men in the EU, the USA and elsewhere.

Although it appears that he/she who watches such race-based pornography has a preference for a certain tribe, this is far from the case, as in the example of Japanese and Chinese women. They are perceived by the Western viewer who fetishises them as being 'less than', 'inferior', 'others', 'inhuman' or 'objects'. Pornography in general is distasteful and unhealthy for individuals and nations, but race-specific pornography is, well, racist, with the viewer either considering themselves superior to the subject or inferior, depending on their psychological health. EU politicians fully endorse this type of racist, dehumanising propaganda pornography; no statement condemning such content has ever been made by the EU and will never be made by the EU.

This brings us to the category of pro-open borders and pro-mass immigration advocates who desire to be seriously hurt by immigrants and immigration. This pertains to First World nations and individuals who are middle or upper class, who have a lot to lose and who derive pleasure from loss or being dominated financially, a rising trend.

And this trend is primarily racist and exploitative, with many of these individuals in the West desiring for as many migrants as possible to enter their lands from the poorest and most war-torn nations as possible, not only expecting (hoping) that they will they be detrimented in terms of paying vastly higher taxation for a myriad of reasons relating to unlimited immigration but also hoping to be physically attacked or worse by the new citizens. This is the racist part; those who fetishise people from the Third/Second Worlds perceive them as lesser than themselves, less sophisticated and more aggressive, which is why they wish to open the borders, in order to achieve pleasure via financial domination, via being attacked, via demographic change and via racially charged conflicts and racial violence.

There has recently been a surge in reported cases of Western "charity workers" (male and female) in refugee camps in Europe (primarily France) having sexual relations with migrants living in temporary accommodations or tents. These are not isolated incidents and these things are not occurring accidentally. There is a subset of privileged and sexually complex individuals who seek to be taken advantage of, especially financially, by those from "lower classes" or from non-Europeans. This has the end result of increasing immigration in order to satisfy the very particular tastes/perversions of the individuals in question, which leaves the migrants baffled but also under the false misapprehension that every Westerner seeks to derive pleasure via financial domination or cultural domination or religious domination—all things that inspire certain individuals to vote yes to open borders because they hope that by doing so they will come to harm in some way.

The 'Fake Nazi'
(Who seeks anarchy and destruction)

Ask a self-identifying Neo-Nazi what could cause a violent confrontation between ethnic Europeans and non-ethnic Europeans in Europe within a decade. He will not tell you, 'Massively decreasing immigration'; rather, he will state that the cause of such an avoidable clash would be even more waves of immigration, which (when combined with high birth rates in migrant communities, inflation, native flight, poverty and pandemics) would result in certain demographic shifts and native dissatisfaction and ever more native flight.

So when certain members of the far right/alt-right complain about immigration, it is as though they are seeking to incite their opposite number (the far left) into doing everything possible to increase mass immigration, which is what they inevitably do—due to the belief that the far left are contrarians. 'Whatever it is, I'm against it!' So even light needling of their opponent causes thousands of red flags to be instantly waved and pro-mass immigration rallies to be hurriedly organised by those motivated not by love of foreigners but by a desire to defeat the far right— their chosen cause, raison d'être, ambition and excuse for not getting their own house in order.

Without realising it, they (leftists/radical socialists/Antifa, etc.) continually 'take the bait' and give the war-and-anarchy-seeking hater exactly what he wants, everything required in order for a real physical conflict to begin, which would destroy Europe. Conflict is not the answer.

The 'fake Nazi' (someone who has never read *Mein Kampf* or the *Communist Manifesto* but who considers himself to be a Nazi (fake Nazi = non-ideological Nazi)) is profoundly unhappy so wishes everyone in his land to become equally unhappy also. He intends to achieve this "harmonising" by pushing the far left to destroy his country whilst he sits back and watches the combined collective pain and chaos. The far left feed off the far right, just as the far right feed off the far left and require them to continue to exist in order to justify their own continued existence, addictions and physical and psychological self-harm. 'There has to be an enemy, doesn't there?'

The extreme psychological and political monotropistic battle between middle-class atypicals and working class atypicals (primarily, middle-class atypical = far left, whereas working class atypical = far right) is the cause of many problems in the West with many of these individuals forgetting altogether that they are individuals, putting themselves second and their obsessive cause (that they become addicted to) first. The end result is a pseudo class war disguised as a battle of conviction and philosophy.

In truth, the majority of those who fall into this category (those who desire ever greater conflict with their rivals) are near mirror versions of themselves in terms of, for instance, OCD, autism and/or ADHD, with only the type and degree of nurture varying slightly. They are almost always 'in it for themselves', locked in a death battle not against the opposing side but against themselves as they refuse to get their own house in order, believing instead that the only solution to every problem in life is war.

The Modern Feminist

Men need women and women need men. We have a symbiotic relationship; we should never be separated or in conflict with one another; we need to reunite. A world without women would be miserable and pointless, but so would a world without men.

Germany has just announced her new Feminist Foreign Policy (March 2023), the same Germany that under Angela Merkel (a proud feminist) deliberately, undemocratically, altered her home nation forever by importing an estimated 1.2 million illegal immigrants in 2015 (many of whom had no ID or proof of nationality and forced their way into Europe), setting an unbelievably bad precedent, which has demotivated hundreds of millions of Africans and Asians from working hard in their homelands due to knowing that they can get a far better quality of life (and an easier one) by simply bullying the Germans into opening the gates to Europe. History has proven that it is folly to bully the Germans; the strict Treaty of Versailles directly led to the rise of fascism and WWII....

When men were in charge of Germany (patriarchy) there were no immigrants headed to Germany; rather, during the first half of the twentieth century, Germany desired to expel every non-German—of course we know how terribly this ended, due to the aggravating factor of WWII.

When women and feminism are in charge of Germany, the exact opposite situation occurs, which seems preferable to deportations and Holocausts (of course) yet results in situations such as:

- 17.3% of the population of Germany being foreign-born (in 2023), who relocated to Germany after 1950, according to the German Federal Statistical Office.

- 19 million people in Germany having an 'immigration history' (19 million people in Germany are 'non-German' in 2023).

- 1.2 million illegal immigrants being admitted within only one calendar year.

- Billions being spent on refugee causes and to fund mass immigration.

These are the results of feminism and extreme socialism.

Many (white European) feminists seek to hurt white European men in any and every way they can in order to get "justice" for past infractions against womankind, with many feminists pursuing the deliberate importation of those who have the least in common with their fathers and grandfathers, which often means importing men who are the complete opposite of a feminist: If feminists get their way in Germany, Germany will almost certainly become an Islamic republic before a century, which will likely lead to the absolute destruction of the feminist philosophy within Germany and a silencing of every vocal feminist voice.

The path Germany is on is one of cultural and societal suicide (or glorious progress and beautiful change, depending on your point of view or if you hate ethnic Germans and Christianity). Those at the forefront of this movement are thinking only of today and of winning the non-existent fight against men, not realising that they are absolutely dooming their own tomorrow.

The German feminist would rather die than live in Iran, Syria or Saudi Arabia but is more than happy for millions of citizens from those countries to move to Berlin tomorrow, arrogantly believing that liberalism, tolerance and feminism will convert these very conservative (patriarchy-centric) religious men into becoming exactly what they desire them to become. They are terribly naïve and are terribly mistaken.

Their actions increase extremism and sectarianism; their actions cause a divide to be created between men and women; their actions do not benefit anyone in the long term; their actions cause native flight and racism—and a renewal of misogyny, which should be decreasing but isn't.

Hitler was bad for Germany, but so was Angela Merkel—and the Jews are today mightily confused because as anti-Semitism massively increases in Germany (in the new feminist and liberal-endorsed migrant enclaves) the Jews are left wondering, *Why were we so hated and forced to wear yellow stars when these newcomers are loved, adored and given everything they demand?*

The key difference here is that Jews in Europe at that time (the 1920s and 1930s) were famously self-sufficient, prosperous, independent and successful, which is why a minority of envious (scapegoating) Germans who wanted to blame someone other than themselves for losing WWI came to hate them. It was Jewish success that caused Jews to be hated, whereas the modern German feminine sympathy for foreigners (or preference for foreigners) is born out of the knowledge that the foreigner has failed in some way or his nation has failed, which causes the German women in question to treat non-Germans as children, seeing them as being unable to help themselves.

This is patronising, but worse is the fact that once the migrant becomes rich and successful in Germany, he will no longer be adored by such left-leaning women because he will have "become the Jew", in effect, and the "love" and kindness we see being expressed by such women in the heart of Europe is reserved for poor foreigners. Woe betide them if they ever become millionaires or billionaires in their new host nation because the liberal feminist wishes them to eternally exist in relative poverty in anti-Israel migrant enclaves in order to ensure she continues to hold the reins of power and authority.

German women feeling sorry for the foreign underdog = guaranteed mass immigration into Germany of low-skilled (or no-skilled) workers, retirees and dependants.

Hitler hated Jews because they refused to surrender to the state (Arbeit Macht Frei = obey the state). Hitler didn't want Jews to become self-sufficient farmers; no, he wanted them all to work for the state, to be subordinate to it). They were heroic and free until the very end, proud and true to their beliefs and identity until the end.

What saddens me greatly, but does not at all sadden the most vocal socialists and feminists in Germany and Europe, is the mass exodus of Jews currently taking place as a direct result of recent mass immigration; there are many examples and reports of this situation.

Jews have been leaving Britain, France, Germany and other nations in Europe in record numbers in recent years, citing anti-Semitism from recently arrived migrants and refugees as the driving factor. However, due to much of the left having a deep hatred and disdain for Jews (due to them insisting on maintaining their identity and separate national status, due to them being self-sufficient, due to them being successful and due to the thorny Palestinian issue) this situation will surely continue until the modern liberal progressives are able to achieve the lofty feat imagined 100 years ago by the NSDAP (facilitated by their demographic change policies)—the complete removal of the Jewish race from the European continent.

Jews are scared in Europe today; European men are scared in Europe today, but at least feminists and liberals are happy, so all is well.

The Profiteer

He could be a specialist asylum lawyer or a hotel owner (whose rooms are used to house illegal immigrants/asylum seekers); he could be a cruel and unscrupulous employer who only employs non-citizens because he knows they will work for pennies due to being desperate and scared; he could be a government translator; he could be a slum landlord; he could be a builder of cheap housing; he could be the owner of the private company tasked by the government to keep order at migrant processing and housing facilities; he could be the head of an NGO whose focus is on protecting and advantaging non-citizens in every way possible. There are many people who profit from mass immigration, from refugees, from illegal immigrants, all of whom will do everything possible to increase the number of incoming new citizens as much as possible for self-serving monetary reasons.

Does the solicitor or barrister who solely represents those who have been denied asylum/refuge desperately care about these individuals from the other side of the planet? No. Rather, he desperately cares about the unlimited flow of money into his bank account made possible solely due to mass immigration.

If every border closed tomorrow, everywhere, thousands of translators, lawyers, slum landlords, people traffickers, employers who operate within the grey economy and all the other categories of people who benefit from mass immigration endlessly continuing would go bankrupt—or would have to find a new way to make a living that didn't involve subverting the will of the majority in order to make a quick buck.

All of these people are short-sighted, they think only of today and only of themselves; they are opportunists, they are taking advantage of the innocents from abroad, they are profiteering from crime and anti-democracy. Illegally entering a nation, climbing over border walls is a crime due to no citizen ever voting for mass immigration or voluntary demographic change and voluntary native flight (reservationism), and mass immigration is, of course, anti-democratic, also known as fascism or minority rule.

When the individuals above are no longer able to financially benefit from mass immigration and demographic change, the numbers of foreign citizens arriving from Second and Third World nations will massively reduce due to the individuals and groups mentioned above being the lure and motivator (in addition to state welfare/benefits) behind many choosing to abandon their homeland in the first place. 'Come here,' they implore, 'come here and you will be rich, loved, housed and taken care of. Come here and we will both benefit. Don't fight against the dictator, no; come here and all your worries and stress will be gone. Come here because we want you to be our underclass.'

The Elites—in sheep's clothing
(Those who pretend they are not elites, supremacists or 'against the little guy')

Fascists are bad, most people agree, because they are dictatorial. They hate democracy and individual rights and freedoms; they put the state first (and elites at the top) and the worker last, whom they dress in a military uniform and throw at neighbouring countries in order to spread fascism and thus increase the wealth and power of the few at the top, the elites.

But we are led to believe (we are gaslighted into believing) that the opposite number of these very bad fellows (the fascists) are lambs, all sweet and innocent, kind, benevolent and trustworthy—the people who carry banners demanding, 'Open the borders; tax the rich!'

They often refer to themselves as anti-fascists or modern socialists, or liberals, or ethical democrats or Marxists. Whatever the name used, the line is always that 'The far right need to be smashed because they are evil and hate democracy. Only anti-fascists and socialists can be trusted to lead the way into a bright tomorrow because we love people, we love workers, and the world will be safe in our hands.'

They would blush if you were to refer to them as being intellectual elites on the left (the proud anti-fascists) due to their raison d'etre being to spend their entire lives trying to convince others that they are liberators rather than users and that they care about rights and freedoms rather than the opposite.

Let's put this to the test.

Ask such ideologically and intellectually motivated (to open the borders) individuals how they would react if every adult in their country suddenly decided to become a self-sufficient farmer, embracing a humble agrarian lifestyle with a limited degree of bartering and trading in local markets.

Would the supremely loving and thoughtful Marxist who desires one big world state applaud and celebrate as he is informed that one and all no longer desire to pay taxes of any kind due to no longer using government services of any kind? Hell no.

Their lifestyle, their elitist lifestyle, necessitates workers—they are the slave master under a new guise, a guise that tricks the naïve and gullible and innocent.

Why are there no anti-fascists working in the fields or down the mines? Because they are marching for open borders in the town whilst waving red flags as they talk to their chums about their latest foreign holiday or promotion at their middle-class job due to the class advantage afforded to them due to their parents being middle-class and them being sent to university.

He who says fascists are bad because they treat the worker terribly and because they keep borders shut is not all that dissimilar. He never wants workers to be free and independent because then he could no longer spend his day like a bourgeois elite reading philosophy and books on politics, strolling through parks or taking bike rides for pleasure rather than as a means to commute to his manual labour minimum wage job.

I see a future where voluntary taxation is not only possible but essential (my guide to this, *Voluntary Taxation*, is coming soon); yet this category of pro-mass immigration advocate would hate this future because he requires taxes. He demands that the class system continue to exist in its present form with everyone else being at the bottom (slaves) and him and only him being at the top (the intellectual superior slave master).

He states that workers are too dumb to look after themselves so the state must look after them, whilst forgetting the obvious fact that the state as it currently exists is an incredibly modern concept born out of inequality and the class divide. No one ever voted for the state; no one ever voted for taxation; no one ever voted for immigration; so who are the real fascists when we consider that the socialists and Marxists and so-called anti-fascists demand that these things not only continue forever but increase massively until the world changes beyond all recognition with only one thing remaining a true constant—themselves remaining on top, intellectual gods who stand above us mere mortals and who direct our paths and fate? Pity the worker who begs to be allowed to be self-sufficient, for he is destined for the gulag....

This category of pro-mass immigration and pro-open borders advocate doesn't fear demographic change because he will not be affected by this change, nor will his career be under threat due to him having a higher education, privileges and advantages that he knows will maintain his supremacy over the vast majority of economic migrants and refugees. Left-leaning elites never fear mass immigration because it only ever hurts and displaces the indigenous working class whilst ensuring a constant flow of workers who will be forced to pay taxes to enable the class system to continue—the main priority of leftist elites (and right-wing elites also, of course).

The (imperial and thus evil) Roman Empire forced ancient Britons to pay taxes to Rome; latterly, kings across what is now the UK chose to continue this trend by forcing Britons to pay taxes to the crown. Fast forward to today and the legacy of Rome and early barbaric kings (whose castles all housed dungeons/torture chambers) continues to linger in a new form, parliamentary democracy combined with an unelected monarch (who has the divine right to rule due to the uniqueness of his blood).

The elite socialist in the UK today (2000 years after the Romans introduced forced taxation on a huge scale throughout the British Isles) has no interest in ending taxation, despite the fact that it has a terrible imperial foundation and has been enforced via the use of torture, murder and imprisonment over many centuries, because, as mentioned above, they would suddenly find themselves working the land and grasping the hammer and sickle they only wish to see on the flags they fly during the endless street protests they are a part of, so long as it isn't raining that Wednesday afternoon when everyone else is at work.

The end result of taxation is always predictable—mass corruption, imperialism, genocide, class divide, and inequality.

Remove taxation and you instantly remove corruption, imperialism, genocide, class division and inequality as these things always necessitate servile taxpayers.

So, ask those who want the state to exist forever, which necessitates tax needing to be paid forever (and who also desire open borders and mass immigration), why they don't instead prefer independence and self-sufficiency—because the end result of their preferred chaotic system will only ever cause native working class suffering and dissatisfaction (depressed wages, higher rents, native flight, demotivation, fear) whilst solely benefiting the few at the top, those who have enough free time to read the collective works of Marx, Trotsky and Engels.

The Guilt/Pleasure/Reward-Driven Christian Zealot

Does he wish to replicate the conditions experienced by early (persecuted) Christians? Yes.

Does he secretly love it when he is banned from wearing a crucifix at his place of work due to offending those he aided in moving to his nation, who he warmly welcomed in? Yes, of course—because when he is persecuted, he feels as though he is a better Christian.

This fellow has a rather complex psychology. He insists on continuing to identify as a Christian, despite knowing about the many crimes and murders, persecutions and pain caused by his religion in the past, from drowning and burning to death innocent women, men and children and cats to the crusades, to the Spanish Inquisition and the subjugation and genocide of native peoples in North/South America.

He feels guilt and shame about these things; however, if he can influence immigration policy by encouraging mass immigration and the admission of every refugee, he feels as though he is atoning. He feels as though he no longer needs to think about all the millions of Christianity's victims if he offers himself, his wealth and his nation as a sacrifice, even risking sacrificing Christianity itself, which in many places is being replaced by new religions, or by atheism as natives lose faith due to native flight and demographic change, overpopulation, wage depression, high rents, etc.

Many might think him a martyr due to being willing to house ten refugees from the other side of the planet who do not speak his language and who viscerally hate his religion and belief system; yet he derives pleasure from these exercises due to it (he believes) washing away the sin of all of those innocent women drowned, wrongly accused of being witches, whilst concurrently guaranteeing his ascension into Heaven. To many Christians (and Muslims) it is easy to become elite and the best of your faith, all that's necessary is to immerse yourself as much as possible in self-abnegation, to deliberately make yourself suffer in every way possible, ever seeking to replicate Jesus' suffering and the suffering of the martyrs, competing with these ancient Christians whose suffering was necessary for the creation of a religion, rather than an artificial exercise in self-harm.

It is because he believes he has 'bought his way into Heaven', due to being responsible for millions of non-Christians entering his nation, causing white flight and his church to be demolished or converted into a dwelling or a mosque due to a lack of native Christians in his area now, that he really doesn't care about what his country looks like or if it will even exist (in singular nation state form) after twenty or fifty years. He does not care about his nation, he does not care about his people, he does not care about immigrants and he certainly does not care about Christians (especially not the ones who avoid suffering and hardship). All he cares about is himself and going to Heaven. He wishes to die as soon as possible in order to escape the tribalism and balkanisation, chaos and demographic change and native flight that he is directly responsible for.

The extreme irony of Christians having sympathy for immigrants who climb over border walls and pay criminal networks obscene fortunes to smuggle them into the heart of Europe is that the Christians themselves claim to hate coveting; yet what is it that drives many of these migrants to move mountains in pursuit of reaching Berlin, Paris and London if not coveting the lifestyles, possessions, wealth and societies of Christian Europeans? Why would Muslims, Hindus and Sikhs choose to relocate en masse to a predominantly Christian capitalistic, class-based nation and choose to fully retain their identity, culture, religion and traditions? What drives them?

The Tinpot Dictator, the Tyrant, the Oppressor of Humanity

Immigrants are mis-sold the West and other countries they are heading towards with promises of prosperity and opportunity. They are never told about the negatives that are pre-existing or the negatives that result from those nations being overburdened by suddenly housing, feeding and caring for millions of new souls who don't speak the language and are so repulsed by the native culture and religion that they choose to self-ghettoise on day one.

This book has identified the many native individuals/groups who benefit from mass immigration and open borders either financially or psychologically (the twenty categories above), yet there also exists a twenty-first type of pro-mass immigration, pro-refugee and pro-open borders advocate. That man is a brutal dictator who hates humanity, who hates his own people, who hates the EU and liberalism but who loves it when entities such as the EU are tolerant and welcoming of immigrants and refugees....

It can be argued that some, perhaps even most, of the twenty categories of native pro-mass immigration advocates are, at heart, good people and not irredeemable or stuck that way for life (one day hippies were everywhere and then they were gone, changed back into 'normal' folk...).

The same thing, however, cannot be argued about the final category of people who support refugees, as many as possible, being resettled throughout the EU, the UK, the USA and elsewhere and the 'doors to the West' being thrown open and eternally kept open.

When an obvious bad guy, someone universally loathed by all, supports the EU's position on migrants, refugees and a soft and liberal approach to handling the migrant crisis, it is time to seriously rethink our collective priorities.

Do tyrants and tinpot dictators (in Africa/Asia) hate the EU's self-harming generous refugee and asylum policies and level of tolerance, passiveness and submissiveness?

No—they positively love these things and they also love the EU.

The very last thing an evil dictator or warlord (the twenty-first category of pro-mass immigration into the EU advocate) would ever desire is for every man and woman to stand their ground. He wants them to flee; he doesn't want them to storm *his* Bastille, so he rapturously loves the EU because the EU takes all of those who hate him or oppose his rule and pays them a fortune in benefits and welfare, which ensures they will never return to reclaim their homeland or liberate their oppressed countrymen and women. The bullying dictator laughs at Europeans for being tolerant as this tolerance and charity for foreigners helps to enable his continuing grip on power, his inglorious rule and his stranglehold on his people and nation.

The One Type of Anti-Mass Immigration and Anti-Demographic Change Advocate/Activist

In contrast to the twenty-one types of pro-mass immigration activists, there is only one type of anti-mass immigration activist—he is a terrified native with little or no stake in society whose voice is ignored by politicians from all major parties.

He is driven by fear. It's in the name of the word he is relentlessly called in a mocking and hurtful way by those who profit from mass immigration—xenophobe.

He is scared, he has reason to be scared, but not of foreigners, no. This man is scared of the twenty-one types of pro-mass immigration advocates because he knows they do not have his best interests at heart and they are the reason why he is once again moving house in search of a new native reservation, further north.

Chapter Eleven — The Benefits of ZeroP, Fast-Track Poly-Interviews and the Reinvigoration of EU Border Security

Internal Benefits

Those who the EU call racist or Nazi or fascist or 'little Europeans' or Islamophobes or xenophobes will collectively be 'defanged' if the EU has sufficient foresight and wisdom to implement the common-sense measures found within this work.

Never want to see a nationalist march again in Europe? Then introduce ZeroP and Poly-interviews; what would such people be marching for after the EU had relieved hundreds of millions of indigenous Europeans of the anxiety caused by the threat of millions of new job, housing and space competitors entering their nation at any moment?

Nationalism and nationalists would become calm; their quality of life, their satisfaction with life would increase massively as rents lowered and wages increased, as depression subsided and optimism, love and hope flourished.

If those (on the left) who claim to be driven by conviction to transform Europe into a blend of Africa and Asia and the USSR are not happy that the native working class are happy (and thus nationalists are now happy), such people can be aided by the EU's new Citizen Exchange Programme (CEP). Within twenty-four hours of making their request, the moralistic, principled, 'One Worlder' with cognitive dissonance who thinks no amount of immigration can ever be a bad thing shall be transported to Syria, Somalia, Yemen or the Congo, where they will finally be happy because they seemingly could never be happy when surrounded by their kith and kin in Europe. I wonder if anyone will miss these people. I'm sure the hundreds of thousands of homeless natives wont.

External Benefits

Say goodbye to dictators everywhere. (France is free because France fought for freedom; Europe is free because she resisted fascism in the 1940s. France is a marvel; Europe is a marvel.)

Say goodbye to mass apathy and defeatism everywhere.

Say goodbye to complacency and irresponsibility and twenty-child families in Africa.

Say goodbye to hundreds of millions subsisting off the charity and goodwill (guilt and masochism) of successful 'die on your feet' Europeans.

What would these millions of migrants and refugees do if they couldn't move to Europe?

They would no longer have the luxury of seeking the help of others to solve their problems and conflicts for them. They would have to stop running, even if that meant marching and demonstrating, even if that meant working fifteen-hour days pulling a plough, even if it meant living in substandard housing with no running water or electricity—because that was the ark of the European, and such hard living, self-sacrifice and profoundly difficult endeavours were the building blocks of the awe-inspiring capital cities of Europe. If one takes shortcuts, they can never be truly happy as they know they are not the cause of their success.

'What are you going to do, join the protest with me and our neighbours tomorrow against the dictatorship or are you going to try to climb over the wall of our EU neighbour again in order to live out your days in one of his decadent supremacist cities of sin?'

If this choice is removed, those who have a pathological hatred and envy of Europeans will no longer be tempted to create even more separatist mini states (future Donbases/future Kosovos) within European cities.

Not a single African or Asian migrant or refugee loves Europe. Why would they? To them it is wholly foreign and its culture 'wrong', 'decadent', 'racist' and 'supremacist'. Migrants only come due to there being better order in Europe, due to the generosity of liberal Europeans, and because they know the EU would never allow Europeans to have a vote or referendum on the issue of immigration, which is why IBTS (the immigration-based tax system) is so crucially important, because the will of all should be known and broadcast, rather than only the will of the few at the top who will never choose to live in a migrant enclave but who insist their fellow citizens should if they were not wise enough to become a politician, celebrity, banker, judge or CEO, the few who are exempt from multiculturalism.

Chapter Twelve — The Citizen Exchange Programme (CEP)

The CEP is an innovative instant solution to the problem of individual natives being angered by closed borders, strict immigration controls, Opt-in taxation, the Right to Buy Food and ZeroP.

The tiny minority of those who will be angered by the implementation of all of these measures concurrently will now have the choice to be replaced by an immigrant from a country of their choosing—one in, one out.

The Citizen Exchange Programme will allow for a 'life swap' to take place between the native Briton, German or Italian and (for instance) a Nigerian, Bangladeshi or Syrian (if those nations are CEP member states).

The indignant, pro-open borders, socialist and 'colour and culture and religion blind' native will no longer feel the need to protest and march, to shout and shriek about the 'fascist' closed borders around his nation because he will be given an immediate exit strategy, allowing him to 'escape fascism'.

The man who will replace him will firstly be vetted (because no nation actively seeks to import, for instance, convicted criminals), and after the vetting process this man from the other side of the planet will be transported to the pro-open borders activist's home, which will become his home, and the native man (after a brief introduction) will then be deported to Congo, Somalia, Mozambique, Yemen or wherever the immigrant originated from, where he will take up residence in his replacement's former dwelling.

Those who complain about ZeroP or Opt-in taxation or insist that illegal immigrants and smugglers pay compensation to the EU now have a means to leave a nation and a system that is so disagreeable to them, with it being assumed that, due to them desiring open borders/mass immigration/ghettoisation in their homelands/balkanisation in their homelands, they will have no objection in any way whatsoever to relocating to any country in the world, in fact preferring to live in those nations that don't have any immigration or refugee restrictions because few if any migrants are attracted to those nations, for one reason or another.

If the pro-open borders and pro-immigration advocate (during a very vocal protest) shouted, 'I want every foreigner to come to Germany but I never want to live in a foreign country,' people would think him mad, absolutely unhinged, or at the very least a hypocrite or someone who viscerally hates his own nation—because if all people are the same and all nations the same, why wouldn't he wish to join the CEP in order to help an immigrant relocate to the West?

Chapter Thirteen — Overpopulation = Solved

Ask Mariam Nabatanzi, who gave birth to forty-four children by the age of forty in her impoverished village in Uganda (she has had three sets of quadruplets due to having a genetic predisposition to hyperovulate, according to her doctor), why she did such a thing. Why has she created a nightmare for future generations to deal with? None of her children can feel special or loved due to the sheer number of them and she cannot possibly be expected to be able to nurture them enough or provide for their needs sufficiently due to her being a single mother. Her individual family unit has come to represent an entire clan, so when the children are a little older, there will exist the very real feeling of these many siblings in this tough environment being a gang.

The mother, when asked, claimed she (recklessly and irresponsibly) created so many new humans due to 'love'. Clearly her mental age isn't high enough for her to be able to make the decision to reproduce. I'm sure someone will disagree with me, but that person, I'm sure, doesn't want to pay for or house all forty-four of these children in their own home/community.

She knows the real answer, at least subconsciously.

If I were to ask her, 'What would have stopped you having so many, over three dozen, children?' she would, no doubt, respond with a smile, 'Nothing, nothing would have stopped me,' which is what migrants on the EU's southern borders say in regards to relocating lock, stock and barrel to Paris, Berlin or London, all wishing to join the great European Gold Rush.

She would say, 'Nothing', but that is not true.

I say to her, 'Imagine the USA disappeared, and the EU and, in fact, every other country in the world disappeared and the only country left was your small country with its very limited, finite resources (many of the products she buys are imported and the healthcare situation is aided by NGOs such as MSF). Would you still have produced forty-four human beings? (Her father produced forty-five by multiple women.) Would you still have chosen to create such a demand for resources, for healthcare, for education, for food, for space?'

Eventually, it would dawn on Miss Nabatanzi that the only reason she birthed so many children is due to the existence of bridges from her land to others, due to Westerners sending aid, sending money and sending medicine to her country and due to her knowing that, worst-case scenario, a dozen or more of her children could emigrate to Europe once her other children and their many, many children consumed all of the local resources.

Yet, it is not the mere existence of successful foreign nations that causes many Africans and Asians to push the world to the brink of overpopulation (birth rates in European nations are decreasing as they are increasing everywhere else); it is the tolerance and liberalism of Europe and the West in general that causes EU citizens-to-be to reject condoms and contraception because there exists a knowingness throughout the world that 'guilt-ridden overly rich, privileged Europeans' will bend over backwards to make you smile, so long as you are not a Christian working-class native Caucasian.

This is the reality; this is why overpopulation exists—Western charity, Western liberalism, Western tolerance, Western saviour complex, Western stupidity.

If you want to save Africa from complete self-destruction achieved via overpopulation and resource depletion, embrace ZeroP. For them and for you the benefit is equal, whereas the detriment caused by the current status quo is also equal. Presently, everyone (apart from big business) loses, whereas with ZeroP everyone wins (with a few exceptions: No more money for sex traffickers or people smugglers).

Miss Nabatanzi's youngest daughter, perhaps now nine years old, is already thinking about starting her own family. The question is do you want her to create two children or forty-two and do you believe ZeroP will increase or decrease the number of children she has and the quality of life those children will experience? (Those who say she should be allowed to produce forty-two children 'if she chooses to' clearly do not care about any of those children individually or about her local community, which is already impoverished and under-resourced.)

If you do not have an opinion about how many children you think she should create, you really shouldn't involve yourself in politics in any way and certainly shouldn't share your opinions about open borders because without rules, responsibility, self-sacrifice, limits and order, we are all just animals doomed to destroy ourselves, and the moment it becomes common for migrants in Europe to have thirty or forty children will be the moment every pro-open borders advocate leaves for a nation where mothers have but one or two children, where there exists a culture of Homo sapienism: practising what we have learnt, being wise enough to prevent future disasters today via the use of self-control, hard work and sacrifice.

Places such as the EU and the USA act as pressure release valves and insurance policies to the Third World, who consider the EU and USA as 'Mommy and Daddy' who will always bail them out of trouble and come to their assistance if they can no longer support the large family they chose to create or if they don't want to build a house or a well or a society worth living in themselves. These words are brutal, I know, but they are true and needed. We need to change.

Chapter Fourteen — There Should Be More Coverage of Indigenous Suffering and Less Coverage of Foreign Suffering

The reason why Europeans must stop themselves from viewing photos or videos of refugees and migrants in foreign lands (in states of distress or claimed distress) is because Europeans are not simpletons, proven by the fact that Europeans conquered the known world. It is unnecessary folly to treat them like children, it is an extreme insult—and much of what we see is propaganda, including the distressing scenes where parents were observed holding their babies over smoky fires in order to make them cry and become distressed, why? Because there was a camera crew in the near vicinity. Footage of this and similar staged events is widely available on the internet, yet those who only watch mainstream media channels will be unaware of the true causes of the tears and the distress.

Europeans know what a man and a woman and a child look like; their lives (in the West) are already terrible. I speak for the majority of human beings on this planet when I say this—do billions pray because they are happy? No, they pray because they are miserable and desperate for change. The Frenchman with no money in the bank, the Englishman facing eviction or repossession from the bank, the German hopelessly addicted to cigarettes, alcohol and cocaine and gambling, which debilitates him and destroys his life, are not all that different or removed from the condition of those who demand entry into Europe. The incorrect perception is that everyone in the EU is happy, with no worries or stress or drama in their lives. This is an extreme fallacy.

Even those with privilege, wealth and a real stake in this world are continually petrified of uprisings, petty crime, envy and the classes displeased to find themselves beneath them.

The emotional effect of exposure to individual cases is only fair if you plan to house, for instance, a family of refugees in your own property.

Emotional imagery and pleas should be reserved for when one individual is asking for the assistance of another individual directly because when one individual makes an emotional plea to the political representatives and influential individuals of another nation, rather than to each individual, the end result is predictable: The representative or celebrity or singer or model or business person is individually touched and moved by the suffering because they themselves wish to avoid suffering and have a great deal to lose so change their view accordingly, which soon comes to dictate policy. However, if they worked in a French abattoir or Italian quarry breaking rocks for sixty hours per week their sympathy for foreigners would disappear. It is only due to being elite and detached (and having unnaturally easy and sedentary lives) that they support migration and the importation of refugees.

(Only those who are not suffering desire to import people from abroad who claim to be suffering, despite suffering already being present all around them in their homeland, which they choose to ignore due to feeling guilty because in order for them to be rich and successful, some natives need to be poor; so helping poor natives (they suspect) would be an admission of wrongdoing on their part, which is why they call them 'peasants', 'little Europeans' and 'knuckle-dragging racists' instead as they quaff champagne and celebrate diversity from their gated communities and guarded penthouses.)

If you see enough footage of economic migrants/refugees on the TV you may turn the other cheek when your government invites one million of these non-EU citizens to live in your country (because you are a good person with a good soul, who cares). But if a man knocks on your door, tells you he's a refugee and asks for money, you will certainly say no (if you have any wisdom or logic or sense of self-preservation) because you only have what you have because you've fought for it, which is why you suspect this man may be deceiving you, because he chose to beg, he chose to flee, he chose to knock on the door, and the fact that he has two babies in his arms only proves that he is reckless and irresponsible because he produced these dependants despite being unable to provide for them.

But even if you didn't suspect subterfuge you would think to yourself, *I am not the richest man in this town, so why should I give this man money?* without realising that the government will be taking money out of your hand and pocket just as surely as if you had given it directly to the man who is banging on your door, disturbing your peace and journey through life, dragging you into his conflicts, depression and apathy, demotivating you and confusing your emotional state, because you have been told you entire life to work hard and be self-sufficient and never to beg.

The state must not be swayed one way or another due to emotive factors; the state must care more about her own people than other people, otherwise the state will not exist for much longer.

Sadly, the modern trend internationally is for political leaders to be almost gregariously emotional; this is due to the stress of the job, fear and altogether too much supremacy and power. The political classes are largely unaccountable, there is a constant recurring universal theme in this regard;

the same is true of the clergy. Strict term limits would swiftly rectify this dangerous situation.

One shouldn't wish for their representatives (civil servants) to be overly 'Borg-like', as such a future is unenviable and that is not what is being argued here, yet it is possible for civil servants to rise above emotions and affectations and thoughts of individual advancement and wealth.

I do not consider this to be a wild dream, especially as we face together the greatest threats our species has encountered hitherto, including of course the war between East and West—please see my book *How We Will Create Peace in Ukraine and the World*.

It is only when our representatives do what they know in their hearts is best for Europeans that the European refugee crisis and migrant crisis shall end once and for all, as currently the percentage of economic migrants that enter European nations is determined not by the will of the people but by big business achieved via political donations and the percentage of refugees that enter your nation is determined not by the will of the people but by the amount of guilt a select few representatives feel after being exposed to pertinent imagery and how much empathy they have for the plight of the individuals in question.

Chapter Fifteen — A 99% Reduction of Migration into Europe (by 2030)

The 99% reduction figure is based primarily on the dual factors of:

1/ The implementation of the 'Immigration Opt-in' democratic and fair tax system (which will communicate to the world that 99% of the population refuse to voluntarily fund migrants or refugee causes in anyway whatsoever because fewer than 1% of people will choose to pay higher taxes when given the choice) and

2/ The uncompromising but fair (fast-track) one-hour asylum/migrant induction process/interview, which will ensure that only genuine refugees will ever set foot in Europe and only then if they are not racist, misogynist or homophobic. Those who say it is okay to import such categories of people should ask voters for their opinion; it will be very, very different.

In addition to these complementary and massively beneficial (for the homeland) measures, the 99% reduction figure is further aided and reinforced via the means of the Citizen Exchange Program CEP (which prevents overpopulation whilst enabling those who hate living in their homeland to emigrate) as well as more practical solutions such as the fleet of (land-tethered) helium and solar surveillance blimps, which will easily ensure not a single human being or animal is able to enter the European Union without the armed forces of the relevant nation knowing about it well in advance. During times of war and international conflict (like now), being relaxed in terms of border security is surely a death sentence, and those who are unable to control their borders are, of course, unable to control their nations.

The Resettlement Lottery will also decrease unwanted waves of migration, due to non-citizens no longer having the luxury of being able to choose what nation they will (effectively) retire to. Once migrants are told that Hungary, Romania, Bulgaria or Poland may be their new 'forever home', many hundreds of thousands, if not millions, will turn around and go home because most desire to live in far more successful and liberal and generous Germany or France—this ends immediately.

For many of the proposals herein to be accepted by the people and their representatives and put into action, it will first be necessary to change public opinion.

This is achieved via the implementation of the wholly democratic measure of 'Opt-in taxation'. If this is blocked by anti-democratic forces, the entirety of this book is irrelevant. We must start with the restructuring of the tax system; all men and women deserve to choose whether or not they pay to actively transform their nation into something they do not at all desire. Paying tax that is used to import new job and housing competitors, which pushes up rents and depresses wages, is a suicidal, self-harming practice, which is why there should be a choice, a simple 'Opt-in' choice. 'If you want to pay the additional 10% immigration tax, place a cross in this box and sign your name to consent to us sharing the fruits of your labours with non-citizens.'

Once this system is in place (the change shouldn't take more than a fortnight) and month on month the percentage of Germans (for instance) who volunteer to pay more tax to fund refugee centres and new housing for migrants and translation and legal costs decreases, eventually approaching 0% of people who choose to 'opt in', public opinion of the non-citizens who continue to try to enter the EU and Germany illegally will dramatically change, which will cause the people to warmly welcome the inclusion of the separate proposals mentioned herein.

Former liberal Germans would say, 'Ninety-nine percent of Germans have voted against any new immigration of any kind by refraining from opting in, so the fact that you are still coming worries us, it angers us, because we know now that you know there is no room or resources here for you, which will mean the quality of life of every German must now decease. Even though we have just proven that we don't want to pay for refugees or economic migrants (because we have already done enough in this regard, not that we had to, because the sins of the father are not inherited by his sons) millions are still trying to circumvent our rules, our borders and our will. Obviously we now need to enact the remainder of Masters' suggestions in regards to ensuring the continuity of the EU and the identity and democratic nature of each individual EU nation.'

If 99% of Germans opted in (to pay more tax individually to help foreigners) every migrant, refugee, fake refugee, people smuggler and user from here to Mars would head directly, immediately, for Berlin.

If, however, only 1% of Germans insisted that they should pay more tax in order to help strangers from faraway lands who likely have no interest in integrating into or adopting German culture, religion or customs, the result would be altogether different. Only the very worst people would try to force their way into Germany thereafter because a 99% vote against mass immigration would be proof positive that the indigenous peoples of Europe are not getting the benefits from mass immigration, multiculturalism and cultural enrichment that they were promised.

Chapter Sixteen — Could European Voters Do More (to End Mass Immigration and Demographic Change)?

Yes. Yes. Yes.

If Europeans truly wanted to end mass immigration, demographic change, the creation of thousands of migrant enclaves and new 'mini states' and the housing of refugees there would be no need for this book because Europeans themselves would have solved these problems long ago and chosen to keep Europe European rather than it coming to replicate the USA in terms of multiculturalism, multiracialism and multi-everything else, which eventually resulted in forced segregation and racism and divides and sectarianism lasting until today in the USA. Or have we forgotten about the BLM riots already? It is risky to mix cultures and creeds, it has always been risky: Look at Northern Ireland, the Balkans, Israel, South Africa, etc., yet still wise progressives are convinced that 'this time' there will be absolutely no fallout or downside from socially engineering demographic change and mass immigration … so reckless, so unnecessarily reckless.

So why doesn't the European voter stop his representatives? Because it is easier to allow someone else to do all of your thinking for you; it's easier to let someone else make your decisions for you, enabling you to spend more free time watching football, drinking away your brain cells or dining at a foreign restaurant—all while you complain about immigration.…

The European's supremacist and privileged lifestyle (the thing that attracts migrants) causes him to refrain from marching, protesting and demonstrating because he loves his modern double or triple-glazed windows and his easy and clean and healthy central heating system; he adores foreign holidays and is bowled over by the new hyper-choice available to him in the internationalist supermarkets that surround him.

His lifestyle and range of choice and freedoms surpasses that of Henry the Eighth or the Caesars or Pharaohs owing to medicine and healthcare, welfare and flawless utilities and modern innovations. He is akin to a living god, able to snap his fingers and have any movie or media displayed instantly on his eighty-inch flatscreen TV, even if he is a virtual pauper due to the 'blessings' of credit and debt enabling all of his bad behaviours and unnecessary purchases. So why would he do anything, say anything, to jeopardise such a fantastic (yet spiritually unrewarding) lifestyle where he can live like a zombie, addicted to caffeine, sugar, salt, cigarettes, alcohol, prescription drugs, cannabis, cocaine, Hollywood movies and football?

He has it 'too good'. He has fallen into the trap of copying the terrible example set by elites, who are drawn towards Rolls Royces and Faberge eggs due to a toxic mixture of greed, vanity, insecurity and lust. This has filtered down to even the poorest Europeans who wrongly envy the super-rich, who wrongly envy idleness, who wrongly believe that football, booze, betting and TV somehow equate to culture, rather than what they truly equate to: irresponsibility, addiction and abdication of power.

The European is choosing to destroy himself with vices that make the few at the top rich (money lenders, tobacco companies, alcohol companies, drug dealers, football team owners, betting shops, casinos, TV manufacturers) because choosing to save himself and his nation would require self-control, a refusal to bow to peer pressure, becoming an individual, becoming strong and becoming willing to make sacrifices for the common good. What sacrifices do football fans make, or casino patrons or technology junkies? Yes, all of these things are choices, but they are choices that destroy not only the European but European culture and eventually Europe herself, which is already changing dramatically—and the average European voter is complicit in its change and demographic transformation.

European will is failing, but it doesn't have to be this way. It is possible for a renewal of responsibility and self-determination, which will in no way look like the Third Reich or a revival of the Third Reich (this thought demotivates many from speaking up) because the hundreds of thousands at the Nuremburg rallies desired the complete opposite of individual responsibility, freedom and self-sufficiency—they wanted one man to do all of their thinking for them. They demanded that one man and one party led them because they feared failure, they feared being wrong, they feared peer pressure and criticism, they feared being free-thinking and courageous, and the rest is history....

It is possible for non-partisan anti-mass immigration protests to be organised. It is not always necessary for this to be a party issue or an ideological issue because if Europe changes much more there will be few or no political parties left due to either the EU replacing parliamentary democracy completely (a one-party continent, akin to the CCP model—the Chinese Communist Party) or radical Islamic republics forming in Germany and France before expanding throughout the remainder of Europe (this is already being called for by many so-called 'Islamists' in Europe and the UK).

This is not an issue for any one party, there should be consensus. All Europeans should want as much power and responsibility as possible, and if they continue to avoid these things, preferring to live the life of an pseudo elite, they will of course be damning their children to an unenviable and inglorious fate of ever greater political corruption, political overreach, complete demographic change and immense voter dissatisfaction. The percentage of those who don't vote should terrify us all because it is proof that the majority culture and philosophy is being rejected by the majority who are fatigued by "social justice", "progress" and inept and unaccountable politicians.

Could European voters do more to improve their situation?

Yes.

Will they?

No. Not until the alcohol, cigarettes, cocaine, anti-depressants, fast-food and gas run out that is.

The European is a willing slave, he chooses an easy life, which he then punishes himself for due to feeling ashamed, but at least he is not a racist or a nationalist.…

Chapter Seventeen — A Conversation on the Border

A Bulgarian border guard who is responsible for preventing illegal immigrants, smugglers, criminals and threats to Bulgaria and the EU from entering Bulgarian territory chooses to speak with one of the migrants on the other side of the border fence, who has been throwing rocks at him and his colleagues all day in an attempt to bully his way into Europe.

After establishing that the young man doesn't speak Bulgarian, Romanian, German, Italian or French, the border guard begins conversing with him in English, the only language the young man is familiar with other than his native Arabic.

Once the young man, who claims to be from Syria but has no proof of this fact, agrees to answering some questions, the border guard asks the first question:

'If you would not tolerate foreigners throwing rocks at you in your homeland, why should we tolerate you throwing rocks at us, in ours?'

The man on the other side of the border does not answer; he merely shrugs.

The border guard chooses now to keep things simple and to start at the beginning:

'How can I help you?' he asks.

'I am going to Germany, please move out of my way.'

'Is Germany expecting you?'

'No.'

'Do you have a passport, a driving licence, a birth certificate, a utility bill or any proof of your identity?'

'No.'

'Do you have employment or housing in Germany?'

'No.'

'Have you visited the German Embassy in any of the countries you travelled through before you arrived here? Have you visited the German Embassy in Ankara?'

'No.'

'Are people allowed to enter your homeland without passports or documents?'

'No.'

'We have the same rules here, why should you be exempt?'

'I am a refugee, I am different.'

'But you have found a refuge and safe haven already, my friend. You now live in Turkey, a safe and modern NATO member. Turkey is your refuge. If you are not happy about the quality of life in Turkey that is something you need to take up with the politicians there, but wishing to leave because other countries are more generous (or masochistic) does not prove you are a refugee; in fact it proves the opposite. Because you are not in imminent threat or danger, it is, in fact, our border guards and soldiers who *you* are putting in danger when you throw rocks at them and at me. Can you please stop doing this?'

'I don't want to live in Turkey, I hate it here. I want to live in Germany.'

'Unfortunately Germany is full. If Germany wasn't full you would already be living there. Germany and France run the EU, they are the mother and father; they forced us to build these walls and fences, they insist that we prevent you from entering our country because France and Germany don't want you to then travel to their countries. They have already accepted millions of migrants and refugees because of Holocaust guilt and liberal guilt. If they had the resources or space to accept more immigrants, why would they be forcing Balkan countries to end the flow of migration from Africa and Asia into Europe before allowing Romania and Bulgaria to join Schengen?'

'No, you are wrong. Germany wants us; Germany needs us. Let us go to Germany.'

'My friend, you have been lied to by somebody, probably people traffickers who wished to part you from your hard-earned money. You are racing towards nations where the political elites, nationalists and Europhiles all agree that there is no room at the inn. You are a few years too late. Perhaps a friend or a relative in the West told you about Western nations giving them free houses and money and such things caused you to say goodbye to your old life and worries because walking across Europe doesn't seem that bad, I guess, when others have painted a picture of bliss and retirement the moment you arrive in Berlin, Vienna, Paris or London....'

'Get out of my way, I have made my mind up, I want the EU.'

'But the EU doesn't want you. Do you know how many millions of Europeans are unemployed and how many millions are disabled and how many millions are non-working pensioners? Do you know how many homes are repossessed every day or how many Europeans are homeless?'

'None of this matters to me. This is not important.'

'It should, it should matter to you, because it is pointless to move to a nation at great physical, financial and psychological cost to yourself when your uninvited presence there will only worsen the local and national social situation. If you want to work, the German or Austrian has a new job competitor; he will not like this. If you don't want to work or can't work, the German or Austrian has a new dependant, and in either case, the housing for additional people doesn't exist, why would it? A man builds one home for his family, not fifteen houses 'just in case' refugees climb over his fence and insist on living with him. Rents will increase due to your presence, wages will stagnate, you will need help and support learning the local language, culture and customs, you will need legal help, you will need translators, you will need healthcare and clothing, furniture and a bank account with money in it....'

'Only racists want to keep me out. Let me in, just me, I love the EU!'

'This isn't about race. If you arrive in Berlin in a private jet with your passport in your pocket rather than a rock intending to employ five hundred Germans in the new factory you are building in Berlin, the first of many such investment projects, what do you think the reception will be from almost every German (socialist, liberal and nationalist alike)?'

'They would like me?'

'They would love you! This isn't about your race or religion or culture or where you come from; this is about resources. They are finite, so those who can contribute the most to EU nations are automatically advanced to the front of the queue. If you were a brain surgeon or a millionaire investor or trader you would already be in the EU with your own EU passport and your own palace in Berlin. You will be asking for free accommodation, yet even if you insist on being self-sufficient and paying your own rent, that will push up local rents in the EU towns and cities, which will hurt the native poor. Is that what you want?'

'But I am happy to share a house with twelve men, no problem. Four men per room, cheaper rent. This won't increase rent for locals.'

'If you were an Austrian father of two young children, would you be happy with twelve men from ten countries away living together in cramped, overcrowded conditions in the next property? It benefits you, only you, from living in such a way—you and the slum landlord you support and sustain that is.'

'What should I do now then, just turn around and forget about moving to Europe? But I've already come this far....'

'"Houston, we have a problem.' Are you familiar with that line? It was spoken by an astronaut from the Apollo 13 crew after discovering a severe fault with their spacecraft, which almost led to their demise. They came so very close to completing their mission (landing on the moon) in the way they planned to, the way they wanted to, the way they prayed to, the way they hoped to—but at the eleventh hour they had to turn back. Just like the man who almost swims the Channel or the man who almost climbs the mountain, the loser is the man who refuses to halt his swim and the man who refuses to accept that the mountain is too difficult to climb and they both die unnecessary deaths after experiencing unnecessary suffering.

'It's okay to try to attempt a thing and not get what you expected because you got other stuff on the way—enriching experiences, passionate experiences, tests of endurance and patience and stamina and courage; but that was then and this is now. Now you need to take one hundred steps back from this border fence. This is my land and my neighbours to the West don't want a single person without ID entering their land. I wish you good fortune on your journey through life, but that journey does not include entering my land. And by the way, drop that rock on the ground immediately. When men threaten my life and the lives of my comrades, I will defend myself. This is your final warning.'

Chapter Eighteen — Language Question

(Relating to the Resettlement Lottery)

Those wishing to enter one of the EU nations, where they plan to live for the remainder of their lives, would be well advised to learn the host language fluently well in advance of their planned migration so they are not excluded from society or disadvantaged.

If a man identifies as a refugee but is concurrently migrating from one region of the world to another, he is migrating, he is a migrant, whereas the physically abused wife in Germany or France is a refugee, due to her not wishing to leave her nation, which is why she seeks protection and refuge in a special centre for victims of domestic abuse—the existence of such places should be mentioned to all migrants who wish to relocate in order to

1/ Reassure them that their host is a caring and loving host and

2/ To provide the most accurate picture possible of their new homeland before they commit to 'becoming European'. When one is standing in a refugee camp in Turkey, Germany must seem like a paradise, yet many women from outside of Europe would be shocked that rape, violence, bullying and abuse of all kinds are an expected everyday part of life in the EU, and homelessness, home repossessions, white flight and self-ghettoisation are as commonplace as corruption, alcoholism, drug abuse, chronic gambling, depression and apathy.

The Question:

'If the EU chooses to share the fruits of the labours of her citizens with you (free housing, healthcare, food, heating and electronic goods, etc.) are you willing to learn their language (the language of those who are always most hurt by a sudden wave of migration, the injection of thousands or millions of job competitors, resource competitors; the native working class)? Yes or No?'

If their answer is 'No', it will, of course, push the applicant to the back of the queue.

(Whichever option is chosen, there is a follow-up question.)

'If you agree to learn (in advance) the language of those who will share the fruits of their labours with you, would you agree to the EU country you will be settled in being chosen at random?'

If the reply is, 'Yes, I agree,' the applicant will be told what new language they need to learn; it could be Polish or Hungarian or French or Romanian or even Ukrainian once the EU has a full presence in that nation.

If the applicant already knows the language of the people they want to protect them and provide for them, their application can be fast-tracked; if not, they can continue the interview process after passing a basic proficiency test in the native language of their new hosts.

It is important to note at this stage that this interview will likely be taking place in the territory of Turkey, a safe and stable nation, a NATO member for seventy years, a safe haven for asylum seekers. It is unfortunate that a delay will occur due to a new language needing to be learnt, yet the long-term advantages for the new citizen and the long-term benefits to the host (no more translation costs or problems in regard to integration) outweigh the need to as hurriedly as possible move person A from Ankara to Bucharest because both nations are allies, friends and partners in NATO.

This process cannot and should not be rushed if the person doesn't understand the local language. Allowing millions to live in the EU who do not speak a word of German, French, Italian or Spanish is madness, this can only lead to further marginalisation and migrant reliance on separate enclaves that represent their homeland or region or religion. If you want Iraq to save you and house you, of course you will want to speak the local language and respect all of the local customs ensuring that you do not offend indigenous Iraqis in any way due to them generously aiding you in your hour of need.

The continuing problem of first and even second-generation migrants in Europe not speaking the mother tongue of their new homeland has been ignored for long enough because it seems weird to save someone's life and then force them to speak your language after they say they want to live in your nation forever; it is a weird and awkward thing to have to do, and because such common-sense measures are not pursued, communities remain divided. Millions cannot and do not feel European because, although being EU passport holders, they don't speak the majority language of any EU nation.

How could an Englishman living in China ever hope to feel Chinese or be accepted by the Chinese people as being anything close to a 'Chinese compatriot' unless he (in advance of relocating to China) became acquainted with their history and culture and decided that he loved it and became fluent in Chinese? He couldn't. The Englishman in China is a tourist until he integrates. The millions of non-EU-born citizens are tourists (or temporary expats) until they integrate. Harmonisation of language, culture and religion is the most common tried and tested means to create social cohesion, peace and order.

If an Englishman wanted to live in China and refused to learn Chinese and refused to integrate with the native people, wouldn't we all call him a racist and a supremacist?

The same rule must surely also apply to those who will accept the EU's benevolent help and protection and accommodation in Europe but do not wish to speak a European language, learn about European culture or Christianity.

If those who claim to be in danger in Turkey (they identify as refugees) refuse to learn the host language and also refuse to be settled in particular EU nations (Eastern Europe and former Soviet Bloc states, for instance) how can the EU approve their claim for asylum? Genuine refugees would be happy to live in any EU nation, surely?

Those who prefer to choose which country within the EU they will be settled in will be considered economic migrants and not those who require the help or protection of the EU. There exists a high level of unemployment and welfare dependency throughout the EU. The EU can make exceptions for genuine refugees, yet if applicants would refuse to ever live in Poland or Romania and would refuse to ever learn Polish or Romanian, why should the EU help in any way or give such people a thing?

If you hate any EU nation or people or language so much that you would refuse sanctuary there, you will never be a happy EU citizen and the only reason the EU would grant you entry would be if every EU citizen was a masochist—and Europeans are not all masochists, far from it.

Chapter Nineteen — Culture Clash

An interview with a prospective EU citizen:

'Are you a religious person?'

'Yes.'

'What is your religion?'

'I was raised to be a Muslim.'

'We don't have enough houses and apartments in Europe, which is proven by the fact that hundreds of thousands of our people are currently homeless. With this in mind, if we give you an EU passport and free healthcare, free housing, free education, free food, free clothing, free translation and legal assistance, would you be willing to share a property with other people due to the problem of overpopulation in Europe caused by recent waves of mass migration?'

'Yes, certainly!'

'Even if the other resident of the property was Jewish?'

'No. They would have to be Muslim.'

'Oh, okay. Well, what if the other resident was a young, single Christian woman who wears short skirts, habitually drinks alcohol and regularly brings men back to her room for the purposes of having casual sex? She will celebrate Christmas, Easter and Lent and doesn't know anything about Islam or the Middle East and never wishes to learn anything about these things now or in the future.'

'No, I will not share a property with such a person. You describe an infidel.... I will need my own property.'

'Why? You said you were fleeing persecution.'

'But the Jewish and Christian and cigarette-smoking and bacon-sandwich-eating people in Europe will persecute me if I am forced to live with them.'

'My friend, no one is forcing you to come to Europe, no one. We are having this conversation through a fence, through a border fence. You can fly over this defensive structure and land in any EU nation of your choice; this is the normal and correct way that European citizens travel. Why don't you have any documents? Why don't you choose to travel in this fashion? No one asked you to come to Europe and no one will force you to enter Europe.'

'I want to live in the EU, but I don't want to change.'

'But if the single woman who wears makeup and short skirts and loves whiskey and beer (who you refuse to live with) wanted to relocate to your homeland and waited for months at the border in her short skirt with a rock in her hand, would you tolerate her behaviour? Would you respect her if she said, 'I want to live in Iraq but I want Iraq to give me my own house because Iraqi culture and social norms disgust me and I don't ever want to change'?

'No, but I am not wearing a short skirt and all I want is—'

'All you want is everything…. Please listen very carefully to what I have to say next. You have stated that you would rather return to your homeland than be given a free room in perpetuity with a sexually liberated liberal Christian German woman who eats pork and celebrates Christmas and who smokes and drinks. You insist that, rather than be housed with her (the person you hate and refuse to tolerate, the young 'pro-refugee' liberal German woman—moving to Germany means living with Germans, with Christians, with Caucasians, with drinkers and smokers and fornicators and drug addicts and atheists) she, as a taxpayer, should be forced to provide you with your own dwelling, completely free of charge.

'Listen to what you are demanding. You are expecting the EU and EU citizens to accept and tolerate you, but this must work both ways. If you are so intolerant and inflexible that you would rather die than share an apartment with a single (dating) Christian female who drinks and smokes, you are not suited for life in Europe, and not only will you be the cause of a rise in radicalism and xenophobia (by your self-ghettoisation), which will detriment you and your family in the long term (because history repeats itself), but you will also be miserable in the short term due to finding yourself living in the next apartment to the woman, who becomes more bitter and hostile to you as the days pass because when she sees you smile, she knows this is due to her efforts and labour. When she sees you have a new phone or clothes or jewellery, she knows she paid for these things. Such an existence is temporary and toxic.

'Even if you said, "But I will get a job," this does not create equilibrium because who are you getting that job from? A native. Would you like it if the short-skirted tequila-drinking Christian German migrant sought employment in Baghdad? Would you be happy if someone who is the literal opposite of you, someone you perhaps intrinsically hate on a deep and guttural and profound level, was able to compete against you for work in your homeland, where your ancestors have dwelt for thousands of years, only able to gain employment in your homeland (during a time of great unemployment) because she was belligerent at the Iraqi border, because she threw rocks and made the Iraqis feel sorry for her because there was a civil war taking place in Europe at the time? You would be mad as hell, but here you are telling me you will work in Germany. If Germany needed workers there wouldn't be a wall between you and Germany.'

'So, you are saying that I am forced to live with whores?'

'No. If you hate that prospect, you can return home, if your homeland is so much better.'

'In some ways it is, in others it is not. I want the EU to help me.'

'The EU is that Christian, alcohol-drinking, liberal, smoking woman.'

'I want her to help me, but I don't want to live near to her, I want the EU to help me.'

'But you insist on what kind of help you are given and how it is given and when it is given. You are not in a position to dictate, and where are your Austrian or Italian or German flags and why are you not speaking these languages also? The languages of the countries you wish to make your 'forever homes'? You are only speaking in English.'

'Why would we speak German or Italian?'

'Because if the German woman was waving the German flag or a flag with a Christian cross on it at the Iraqi border and was joined by hundreds of thousands of others with similar flags and none were speaking Arabic but, for instance, English, wouldn't you view such an occurrence as an invasion or a crusade?'

'Yes, but this is different. I don't wave a Muslim flag.'

'But you are speaking only in English to me and to journalists. No one here is speaking German or Italian or French, you are shouting loudly in English that you demand to be relocated in non-English-speaking countries while insisting that your very different culture and religion be accepted, welcomed in, tolerated and given more than equal freedoms, representation and rights within the host nations. How would you feel if you were a tolerant Christian German man listening to a Muslim Arabic-speaking Iraqi man shouting loudly in English demanding to be allowed to enter Germany with one or two million other men very much like him?'

'I don't know how I would feel.'

'That's the problem. You need to put yourself in their shoes because, if you don't, there will be more ethnic conflicts and religious wars in Europe. No one in Europe wants this. Do you not understand you are not entering lands that have known eternal peace? You are entering lands that have only known war and conflict and tribalism, which you only gravitate towards due to them seeming less corrupt, less violent, less chaotic and less depressing than your homeland; but Europe will not remain the same if she becomes more like you, if she prioritises you and your needs and wants and puts Christians, drinkers, smokers and short skirt wearers last, because Europe would no longer be Europe, and the socialism and liberalism that created generous welfare systems will also be gone.'

'One more person will not make such a difference, I am only one person.'

'But there are millions behind you who will follow you to Vienna or Berlin—millions who should be fighting dictators and bullies and apathy and pessimism and nihilism and self-weakness. If the many millions who have already decided that 'it's the EU or nothing' for them (who have already burnt every bridge) stopped running towards cities they hate

(Christian, capitalist, drinking culture, Christmas etc.) in search of 'salvation' and turned around, who would have the ability to stop their awesome combined will? No one. What is harder, returning home and getting your house in order or being a flatmate of a very sexually liberated Christian woman who (due to race/class/privilege/guilt) sends 30% of her wages to Oxfam and Amnesty International each month?'

'I don't know. I honestly don't know.'

'Think about what I have said, my friend, because winning today may cause absolute defeat tomorrow, and it is truly meaningless to stand in the middle of Berlin with a German passport in your hand. It does not mean you are now invulnerable and bullet proof and saved forever and guaranteed to be loved and protected by Germany and Europe because German Jews all had German passports in the 1930s and 1940s; they were all German citizens, but rather than guaranteeing their safety and freedom, these very things guaranteed that they would be persecuted, humiliated, enslaved and dehumanised. (Citizenship is not always a good thing; it means that you are owned by the state, especially during times of war.)

'If you are not yet fluent in German, get fluent in German (before attempting to enter Germany). If you haven't yet asked Germans if they want you there, do it, ask Germany if they want additional citizens this year—and if you don't ask this question, do not be angry or surprised if you suffer xenophobia in Germany. You should only wish to live where you are wanted, welcomed and loved. Why would you want to live where you are not welcome and why would you want to live in a place surrounded by people you cannot or refuse to tolerate? For instance, hundreds of thousands of single women who drink and smoke and eat pork, who wear makeup, who don't wear veils and who never ask a man for permission for anything.'

Chapter Twenty — Questions from a Taxpayer

An EU voter and taxpayer asks his government a few questions regarding 'Immigration Opt-in'.

'Hello, can we please introduce an Immigration Opt-in tax system in our country?'

'No.'

'Well, in that case, can we have a vote instead on mass immigration and the resettlement of refugees and the sending of our wealth and resources to other nations and to other peoples?'

'No.'

'Could I please ask why?'

'Because Europeans support immigration and helping refugees here and abroad, these are our values.'

'How do you know Europeans support these things? There hasn't been a vote.'

'Only fascists hate refugees and immigrants.'

'The only thing I hate is there not being enough democracy or accountability in my nation. If you were convinced that Europeans support these progressive causes and ideas why wouldn't you allow Europeans to vote in a referendum on this issue and on the issue of continued membership of the European Union, unless you are scared you will hate the results? Do you hate democracy?'

'No one wants to leave the European Union, why would they?'

'Ask Britain that question. If one million people asked you to change the tax system, to make it an Immigration Opt-in system, would you?'

'No.'

'Five million?'

'No.'

'How many people need to request this change?'

'It is not about numbers, we will never allow taxpayers to choose how their contributions are distributed across the world.'

'And the referendum on immigration and on EU membership; if ten million people wanted these referendums (because you refuse to ever so slightly tweak the tax system) would you allow taxpayers to have their vote and their say?'

'No. Our values and principles are unchangeable. If you want more democracy and referendums, the EU will cease to exist.'

'But I thought the EU was a democratic institution designed to help the native peoples.'

The EU exists to help all peoples; the EU is not racist or selective. You are no different than an African or Asian man, so why should your voice be louder than theirs? Are you racist?'

'I didn't say I am better, I just asked for a referendum because the EU has changed over the years, it in no way resembles the EU of a few decades ago, when it was the ECC (created in 1957 to 'foster economic integration among its member states'). No one, in fact, not a single European ever voted for the European Union, this is the creation of unelected bureaucrats and elites. Can I please opt out of funding mass immigration and demographic change and sending the fruits of my labour abroad?'

'No, but if you are not happy you can leave the EU.'

'Are you sure that blocking the Immigration Opt-in tax system is the right course of action? Every taxpayer is able to tick the box that states, 'I want to opt in to fund every refugee and migrant cause that my elected representatives want me to fund,' so what's the harm? Won't everyone tick the box?'

'But what if no one chose to opt in? Who would help foreigners then?'

'They would have to help themselves, but maybe a few thousand taxpayers would choose to pay more tax, the uber-masochists and self-haters among us, which should be their choice and right. Just as it should be my choice and right not to pay higher taxes to fund migrant and refugee causes, translation and legal costs, accommodation, welfare, healthcare and all the rest of it.'

'No, you are wrong. Most EU taxpayers would warmly welcome the opportunity to pay more taxes in order to help migrants, so if we granted your request for Immigration Opt-in taxation you wouldn't be happy because only a tiny minority would opt out of funding our progressive and liberal ideological internationalism.'

'So, will you change the tax system?'

'No.'

'But you said most people would choose to pay more.'

'Yes, which is why we don't need Immigration Opt-in because we already know the result because we know how Europeans think and we know what is best for them.'

'Is that the same reason why you don't allow taxpayers to vote on immigration and EU membership?'

'Exactly! Because it would be a waste of time and money, and in any case, Russia would try to interfere in the referendums, or the USA would or China would. There would be election interference, which is why we should have as few votes as possible because democracy can easily be "hijacked".'

'Are you saying that the best thing for me to do is not question anything or complain because there will never be a vote or referendum or change in the tax system and that the many millions who want more democracy should emigrate if having their voice heard and their will enacted is so important to them?'

'Yes, yes, exactly. Anyone who criticises anything the EU does is not welcome in Europe; they are the enemy of progress and liberal democracy. Goodbye.'

Chapter Twenty-One — Europe Needs Pioneers, Not More City-Dwelling Consumers

If every migrant and refugee currently attempting to relocate to the EU desired a few acres of land, some timber to construct a house and a stone to sharpen their axe and scythe, even the most ardently nationalistic German, Italian or Hungarian would be forced to respect these newcomers because if that was the shared intent, if the millions who wish to settle in Europe were all pioneers akin to those who crossed the Atlantic and 'won the West', many Europeans would feel humbled.

There are, no doubt, many farmers and labourers, manual workers and tradesmen and women of every stripe around the EU's borders who desire entry plus citizenship; however, none expect to be relocated in the countryside. None of them expect to ever see a plough or axe or farm or a harvest taking place as what the EU citizen-to-be desires is not the self-sufficient and strenuous life of a provider and labourer because they wish to unnaturally leap ahead (in terms of class and caste advancement), becoming instant members of the 'urban pro-big-state welfare class'; those who disagree with this assessment are in denial about the reality of the situation.

If those who wish to rely on the EU for protection and sustenance were offered free parcels of land in the EU, rather than free apartments in Berlin or Paris, how many takers would there be? Few to none, sadly, as those who are happy to relocate to a state within a state (living in the EU) are clearly not driven towards self-sufficiency, independence, responsibility and accountability (because the EU does your thinking for you and gives you free stuff). It is easier to live in a modern and advanced Western city surrounded by supermarkets, cinemas, restaurants, casinos and brothels than it is to live a few miles out of the city surrounded by agriculture, toil, hard work, nature, responsibility, independence and freedom.

European nations should be encouraging their own people to leave the city rather than causing the city (and thus urban, liberal, supremacist and elitist culture) to further spread and grow like a nation-destroying cancer, causing great disenfranchisement and a divide between 'the Romans and the Plebs'. As mass immigration causes towns and cities to grow at an unnaturally exponential rate, it will only guarantee one thing: future mass unemployment due to virtually every newcomer making themselves vulnerable to change due to choosing not to be self-sufficient and opting instead to be a pseudo-middle-class privileged and protected individual in the city rather than an independent and free man in the countryside, who proudly feeds himself and his family.

The time bomb is ticking; complete dependence on the state is the ruination of man and the enabler of authoritarianism, totalitarianism and fascism. Men in the EU (if they want Europe to exist a century from now) need to spend less time in European cafes, bars and concerts patting themselves on the back and celebrating their supremacy, success and abundance of leisure time and wealth and more time working the land, felling trees for furniture and firewood and defending their land with the strength of their chests and the will of their hearts as they gradually move towards paying a 0% rate of tax and thus becoming free. Citizens who take nothing or little from the state should pay nothing or little to the state. Only fascists and envious thieves disagree, ignore both.

What irks so many about modern mass immigration into the EU is that the vast majority's preference when arriving in Europe is to automatically head in a drone-like fashion to the biggest/wealthiest city—the NYC effect.

In tandem, due to generous liberal welfare systems in Europe (created for the sole purpose of providing support for the indigenous poor of Europe) millions of 'new citizens' throughout the big cities of the EU become adopted and kept for life, with welfare dependency in this demographic being far higher than it could be, than it should be. If the will was there to create a truly fair and equal Europe the statement 'Citizens First, Non-Citizens Last' would be common sense and would guarantee social order was maintained at home, whereas the statement (which seems to be the viewpoint of the majority of EU politicians) 'Non-Citizens First, Indigenous Working Class and European Poor Last' is guaranteed to push the Union to breaking point, after a few more Brexits first, of course.

The end result of the importation of millions of new city-dwelling elites is that they will almost certainly adopt the general personality and psyche of the city, which will have already been the cause of great disconcertment among neighbouring native communities over a period of many years.

A native tolerates another native's 'supremacy signalling' because both of their grandfathers battled the Nazis, for instance, so the white working-class man born and raised in a village turns the other cheek when the white middle-class man born and raised in the city makes it abundantly clear that he thinks non-city folk are 'peasants', 'inferior' or 'plebs' (because he feels guilty for standing on their backs, he would prefer them to be robots). The native villager already knows the supremacy and elitism of the city are threats to him, yet the fear and feeling of inferiority and insecurity this causes are not soothed by millions of non-European city dwellers relocating to the cities around him; such an occurrence of course (as European history proves) has the opposite effect.

The EU needs to be more than cities and rules and principles alone if it wishes to survive; there needs to be real purpose. Men need to be more than mere numbers and men need independence, liberty and control over their lives. The EU's confidence has got it this far, yet henceforth she will need to make the case to her many millions of indigenous citizens of the importance and urgency of making Europe more multicultural and diverse as quickly as possible and increasing the size and power of liberal cosmopolitan cities and massively increasing state dependency and welfare dependency whilst dramatically increasing taxes.

Chapter Twenty-Two — Demographics, Native Flight, Progress and Tolerance

There seems to be an acceptance within the world of middle-class liberal privileged folk, who live far from any of the ghettos or migrant enclaves they have helped to create, that demographic change, mass immigration and native flight are all very good and progressive things—because it is the native poor, the liberals and progressives claim, that are the problem....

Firstly, about progressiveness; despite what many wish to believe, progressiveness does not mean maintaining the current order as it exists, for instance tolerance, 'one world', social benefits, pensions, minimum wage, abortion rights, etc., as, by definition, the word progress suggests and demands constant change. I can understand those with the loudest voice in 2023 believing that the changes they have helped to usher in to make the world a better environment for themselves and their needs, wants and tastes will forever now remain unchangeable, yet this is not the final form of society or way of life because the moment the progress and change halts, those with the most power and influence will be deemed by the majority to be fascists. There was a time when unions only existed to help native workers; now they help and facilitate the mass importation of competitors for their own members in many nations, becoming the tool of their own destruction due to giving bosses exactly what they want: an unlimited supply of cheap labour.

This is but one example of the unexpected consequences of glorious change and progressiveness. The welfare and social benefits that exist in the UK, for instance, were hard won, by native people for native people, yet as soon as natives (via progress) forced a change in the system, winning concessions such as free healthcare, pensions, state housing and minimum wage, predictably, millions of non-natives were drawn to the UK in order to enjoy the rewards hard fought for and paid for by a hundred generations of working-class Britons who had been slaves to elite power in the British Isles. Brexiteers are those who remember this history; Remainers are those who want this history to be forgotten.

Chapter Twenty-Three — Tolerating Demographic Change

Native flight is a natural reaction, yet those with privilege, who are untouched by mass immigration (a trickle of new faces doesn't rock the boat, but millions within a short period does) call this phenomenon racist and demand that the native working class be more tolerant and celebrate diversity. Yet, when we apply this same rule to other cultures, races and regions, these same individuals quickly change their tune—which reveals either their hatred of the indigenous European working class (because they are unruly, and so they should ever remain!) or, more likely, the fact that they are supremacists hiding behind the mask of tolerance and multiculturalism, who benefit in every way from mass immigration, which necessitates them using any and every weapon against the only people who benefit from it in no way whatsoever, the native poor.

Let's compare Plymouth in the UK with the first English settlers who arrived in Plymouth, USA.

2023 in Plymouth, UK: A white progressive middle-class privileged liberal lecturing the native poor (native Britons).

'What do you mean you want a democratic vote on immigration? Are you a racist? The people coming here are no different than you, you should love them, embrace them and be friends with them; you have absolutely nothing to be afraid of.'

1620 in Plymouth, USA: A white progressive middle-class privileged liberal (after time-travelling back) lecturing the native poor (Native Americans).

'What do you mean you want a democratic vote on immigration? Are you a racist? The people coming here are no different than you, you should love them, embrace them and be friends with them; you have absolutely nothing to be afraid of.'

Doesn't this sound strange and a little bit spooky? It is perfectly acceptable for the white progressive liberal to berate, bully and lecture poor whites, but when he does the same thing to poor Native Americans as hordes of European immigrants arrive, it doesn't seem quite as acceptable, does it? Why? Because it seems like self-serving bullying because he is the same race as the incoming immigrants.

'Xenophobe' is a bad word, yet if all Native Americans had been xenophobes, they would still have a country today, rather than humiliating reservations. This is why Britain voted for Brexit, in a desperate attempt to avoid this same fate. It is only natural to wish to survive and thrive, rather than be forced to flee, move, and gather in reservations for safety … until the elites start another war, of course, and force you to be their cannon fodder again.

The lesson here is it is okay to bully certain natives but it is evil and reprehensible to bully other natives. Who makes these rules? Liberal progressive zealots who desire complete dominance, who exist in a twisted alliance with big business, slum landlords and asylum lawyers.

I want these same enforcers of tolerance and enforcers of multiculturalism (an unnatural model and unsustainable without eternal strict government control and an ever larger state) to travel to Papua New Guinea or the North Sentinel Island or the forests of South America where untouched indigenous tribes can still be found.

I want these enforcers to travel to these lands and take with them a million members of the white working class from European countries. I want these liberal heroes to look into the eyes of the tribesmen and explain that it would be racist for them to do anything other than smile when they see the tribeswomen flirt with the European men. I want them to criticise the tribesmen for thinking about fleeing when the Europeans bring new languages, culture and religions. I want these enforcers to loudly espouse the virtues of the natives' ancient and unique culture suddenly becoming second or third or last fiddle. I want these liberal progressives to "educate" the natives about the need to learn all about the new cultures and religions as they are forced to translate official government documents into European languages and house white refugees and tolerate endless 'white lives matter' marches.…

Anti-white working-class zealots will, at this point, say, 'But white people once colonised and raped and dominated non-white people … so fair's fair' (whataboutism). No, fair is not fair because those things were ordered by elites and only benefited elites and the middle class. The white working class were slaves at that time also, working sixteen-hour days in factories, suffering terrible injuries operating dangerous machinery, and the children therein often receiving beatings from managers and foremen, all while living in overcrowded slums in conditions that severely damaged their health or, worse, workhouses.

For instance, the left-wing Remainer Benedict Cumberbatch's ancestors owned many slaves, his family benefited in the past from slavery and colonisation just as he and his family continue to benefit to this day from the atrocities of the past due to the wealth created from owning slaves and plantations—you only know his name because he was born into privilege as a result of the crimes of his ancestors, his education paid for by the victims of his ancestors. In contrast, every white working-class Brexiteer is born into poverty, which is why he is anonymous, which is why he is blameless for the sins of elite white families.

When the native is a poor European, it is okay for him to be bullied, humiliated, degraded, forced out of his ancient settlements, forced to pay higher taxes to fund mass immigration and the housing of refugees, and forced to pay higher rents due to overpopulation; it is okay to berate him and call him a racist and a bigot and 'worse than Hitler' for disagreeing with liberal progressive ideology. No, no, no; it's not okay; this must end immediately if we wish to avoid terrifying conflicts erupting in Europe and beyond, caused by the long-term subjugation and marginalisation of the native poor and underprivileged, which some would term bullying. I call it evil. I want to ensure these conflicts do not occur, do you?

Unfortunately, the middle class and elites will need to take a pay cut in order to ensure the survival of us all. That champagne, that second property, that exotic holiday costs more than you know.... You are damning your own future.

If you wouldn't expect working-class Chinese villagers whose culture has remained constant for untold centuries to celebrate and cheer when churches and English pubs and cricket and European culture and European languages were forced into their village all of a sudden, without warning and without a vote, don't expect German, French, Belgium, Polish, Hungarian or English villagers to cheer and celebrate when they experience the very same things without a vote, without a say, as this is racism, this is bullying, this is incomprehensible madness.

Chapter Twenty-Four — 'Hey, Foreign Beavers, Why Don't You Abandon Your Dam?'

A tribe of beavers are building a dam, they are two-thirds of the way across the raging river when a few of the beavers, who don't like being buffeted by the river and who don't like getting wet and are unhappy about being cold, begin to complain about having to complete the difficult and perilous task.

The majority of the beavers tell the few unhappy beavers to stick with it and persevere, saying, 'Separately we are weak, but united we are unstoppable!'

As the minority of beavers ponder what to do, they hear the cries of foreign beavers, from many rivers away, declaring that their dam is already built, that their beaver society is happy to accept all those beavers who have no interest in building dams and remaining united in their home rivers, who are invited to live and work in the already built beaver-dam paradise, which features a blue flag flying overhead, with stars formed into a circle, representing that there is unity and conformity there.

The offer of being able to move to a ready-made dam is too much temptation for the beavers who complained about being responsible for building their dam, so they declare that they wish to leave their native beaver community forever, choosing to abandon the dam-building project, opting instead to become refugees who will go in search of a new tribe of beavers to take them in. The first tribe they will ask for help, housing and protection will be the tribe with the blue flag with stars on it because their dam seems very strong and secure and is a long, long way away, which will ensure that they will never return to their home river because the journey is too far to endure twice, this is a one-way journey only.

Predictably, their absence causes the dam in their home river to fail, destroying the defences of the beavers because there weren't enough beavers left to complete the dam. The river completely destroys the dam and, afterwards, destroys the beaver village also.

Psychology of sympathy for refugees: I will use the example of a politician who is a vocal pro-refugee advocate who wants millions or tens of millions of refugees to share in the fruits of his labour and the fruits of the labour of everyone else in his homeland.

When politicians say that all citizens should desire to love refugees and accept as many refugees as possible into their nation, into their welfare systems and even into their homes, they are not saying this for 'good Christian reasons' such as charity, being a 'Good Samaritan' or other core components of that religion, which most Europeans are familiar with.

Rather, they are communicating a psychological instruction due to the consequence of the decision to accept refugees—that being the revolution that could have happened if there was a wall built around the country in question, which was prevented due to seemingly benevolent or masochistic or opportunistic actions—big business desires new customers, the middle class desires cheap workers, big business desires to stagnate wages and slum landlords seek to increase rents.

The politician, naturally wishing to remain in power even if he makes mistakes, and we all make mistakes, we're all human, knows that in order to increase political power and state control it is necessary to give the people a glimpse of the potential end result of their attempt at taking on the state. (When refugees from a war-torn country are living next door to you, your mind is ever on the suffering you imagine they experienced with their very presence being a vigilant reminder to keep your head down, pay your taxes and keep voting for the people the polls say are going to win.)

The big disincentive for desiring individual responsibility, a greater stake in society, is the example (having open borders) of the potential future fate of the indigenous taxpayers should they ever attempt to divorce politicians, politics and state power.

Further, taking in refugees gives the general impression that if you are dissatisfied it's easier to leave your shores because some 'kind country' will take you in than it is to launch a revolution.

Thus, the EU is willing its citizens, if disgruntled, to leave (for the US, Australia etc.) rather than engage in an uprising.

The terrible irony of this situation is that due to those who usher in such liberal agendas as open borders not living near refugee centres or minority quarters of towns or cities, they have long been unaware of the building xenophobia, which now, having been allowed to fester with genuine concerns not being addressed, threatens to disturb the peace and threatens social order, things every citizen must fight to preserve. Listen to no man who tells you to fight another; use your own judgement. Always choose peace and dialogue wherever possible, but always defend yourself.

The EU is basically saying they don't want to encourage a Tiananmen Square or the guy who stood up to the tanks in the iconic photograph; instead, they think this man and these students should have left China as refugees and not tried to change their country. They are preaching surrender to all citizens, everywhere, on planet Earth.

If the EU had existed during the time of the French Revolution but France was the only nation not in the EU, an interesting and terrifying thing would have taken place. The EU, due to having a very liberal immigration and refugee belief system, would have accepted hundreds of thousands of starving French men and women, the same men and women who would otherwise have fought and won the French Revolution.

The only reason France is what she is today is due to no other nation offering to house, feed and provide healthcare services to millions and millions of French men and women, most of whom wouldn't have arrived with ID documents or even proof that they were from France.

If men from Spain heard that millions of Frenchmen were getting free houses, cell phones and dental work all thanks to the German taxpayer and their bizarre liberal refugee programme, of course many Spanish men and women of that day would dress as their French neighbours, would learn a few words of French and continue shouting, 'I am a refugee, protect and help me....'

If a French man or woman was heard shouting that phrase before the moment of that nation's revival from tyranny, the revival never would have taken place.

Fighting back against bullies is hard. The Russians fought and won their revolution, so did the French, so did the Americans, and even as a Brit I can't help but be proud of the Americans for standing up for themselves to a far more powerful colonial power.

The USA is called the land of the free for one reason and one reason only: because when the Red Coats came with bayonets fixed, the Americans answered with clenched fists rather than declaring they were refugees and seeking protection from her neighbours to the south.

What France, America and the EU are saying (via admitting refugees) is, 'Although it took great sacrifice and martyrdom to win the freedoms all of our citizens enjoy, we don't want you to have to put in the same effort we did against the British Empire or when we fought against the Roman Empire or when we fought against the Third Reich.' This creates refugees and refugee problems and waves of economic migration. This has the end result of undermining all Second and Third World nations, of demotivating beavers everywhere.

What the West is saying is it doesn't matter if foreign beaver dams fail due to their attractive Western liberal generous welfare systems and tolerance enticing beavers away from work and toil towards the bright lights of the West—which has already built modern dams, already done all the hard work.

The question is, is the West deliberately causing all of these foreign beaver dams to fail or is this merely an unfortunate consequence of their hubris, supremacy and liberalism?

Chapter Twenty-Five — In Defence of Romanian and Bulgarian Border Guards

When liberally minded EU individuals see a burglar at their window, do they spend ten minutes on the phone to the police imploring them to be gentle, tolerant and peaceful when they arrive or do they say, 'Get here now, bring every damn weapon you have. Please save my family and defend my resources and peace'?

To ensure Western EU politicians can enjoy the full international experience and "cultural benefits" of mass immigration and also to help aid them in understanding the problems facing those guarding EU borders, I suggest rehousing liberal EU politicians (at all levels) in the migrant enclaves they have chosen to create within every EU town and city.

When you live in an ivory tower with ivory-tower-esque people, you will call East Europeans racist when their police officers 'keep out foreigners'; however, if the same ivory-tower EU politicians couldn't choose where they lived, if the people insisted that they only reside in multicultural refugee quarters of their towns and cities, they would very soon learn empathy. They would understand why the term culture clash exists and they would perhaps feel different about identity and the importance of good neighbourliness if suddenly they found themselves in a place in their own nation where their language isn't spoken, where their religion isn't practised, where their morals, ethics, principles and virtues are openly attacked and spat on, and where the welfare/benefit/legal systems the representatives created for good have been co-opted by every man and his dog from near and far in the interests of

1/ Forever remaining separate.

2/ Forcing the local culture to change—to suit the incoming cultures.

3/ Becoming 'kept' due to belligerency, bullying, being pushy, climbing over borders and walls and fences and rules.

Yes, suggest this idea at the next EU meeting. I wonder how many 'pro-immigrant' (whatever that means) EU politicians would smile if told they could no longer live in their very European and very white gated community or their protected and lavish penthouse apartment? Not one of them because they only want others to benefit from the chaos that is multiculturalism. When, suddenly, twenty languages are being spoken in your local market, all would agree that is the definition of chaos and disorder and bound to cause anxiety to all.

If native working and middle-class men and women (from Britain to Norway, Sweden to Germany, Italy to Greece and Spain to Austria) feel the need to engage in white flight, who genuinely believes that Green Party or Liberal Party EU politicians would be able to remain and tolerate being a minority in migrant enclaves (basically foreign lands)?

Those who yearn for this are hyper-masochists or don't know why there are only a handful of Native Americans in existence today whereas previously they were many—who possessed their nation rather than a few acres called 'reservations'.

It is hypocrisy such as this (forcing voters to tolerate the lifestyle that elites/politicians reject) that helped push the UK away from the European Union. It is pushing Hungary away; it is pushing Romania and Bulgaria away and is demotivating all others into wanting to join also—Serbia recently announced (via polls/public mood) that she has no intention of joining the EU in the near future. This negative feeling towards the EU will only continue to grow until the indigenous peoples and their right to protect and preserve their culture, identity, faiths and borders are protected at every level of the EU.

Don't call these new EU nations racist for defending their nations if you don't also call Ukrainians racist for defending their lands.

If 1,000 men are throwing rocks at you or 1,000 soldiers are throwing grenades at you, what's the real difference? Both events can trigger casualties on both sides and an increase in anxiety, stress, xenophobia and depression in the homeland.

An attack is an attack—the Balkan nations have not invited these large groups of aspirational EU citizens to their frontiers. They have absolutely nothing whatsoever to do with these individuals who aren't neighbours, who aren't allies, who are in no way attached to border guards other than being fellow human beings.

If you ask a man from another tribe to your land and then attack and mistreat that man, everyone will call you a racist, evil, a fascist and such like. However, if you have not invited the man from another tribe to your land, if he arrives one day with a rock in his hand, no passport, a great measure of rage and frustration and a desire to subdue your will, to defeat your laws and your security apparatus, how can you be called any names whatsoever when you put the protection of your people and nation first by ensuring such individuals are eternally kept out?

Those who cry racism or supremacy the most tend to be the most racist and most supremacist; this is psychological projection. The devil is the accuser.

Chapter Twenty-Six — Rock-Throwing and the Schengen Union

If I throw a rock at anyone, I accept that my life is forfeit because I have just committed an act of attempted murder.

It does not matter if I am angry and hungry. If you woke tonight and found me standing in your bedroom with a rock in my hand, would I be justified in throwing it at your sleeping face because you have more resources or because your house is in my way and it is preventing me from getting to the German house next door whose confused occupants throw money at me when I throw rocks at them, who are real pushovers, so much so that I lose all respect for them? No.

If you arrive at someone's property without a passport, without a CV, without a suitcase, with only a mobile phone and a balaclava and expect to be allowed to enter, you are certainly not the type of person that individual, community or nation wishes to be anywhere near their property. Only those who respect sovereignty and recognise and respect the right of individuals and communities to own and defend land and property should be considered for admission.

The young Syrian man who wishes to become a German citizen (because Germany and the EU are "generous", giving free housing, healthcare, education and money out as if they were candy rather than the fruits of German labour) would not have smiled and been relaxed and tolerant if he witnessed tens of thousands of young Romanian, Bulgarian and Hungarian men, armed with rocks and knives, who were wearing balaclavas a few miles away from his ancestral village in Syria (in peace time, before the most recent conflict in Syria) as they attempted to invade his nation.

The Syrian throwing rocks at the defenders of the EU on the Turkish border today would have certainly, unequivocally, also thrown rocks at each and every European "refugee" who dared try to force their way into Syria, who dared attempt to drain Syria's welfare system or social housing, who dared attempt even to use that proud nation as merely a bridge in order for the mob of EU refugee men to then force their way into other nations, nations they preferred due to them being more liberal, more tolerant, more generous: more masochistic, self-hating, disunited and self-harming.

Or are we to believe that those who throw rocks don't care if hundreds of thousands of undocumented men roam through their nation, disordered, a sovereign power akin to an army or mini state with organisers and people traffickers heavily coordinating clashes and movements?

Of course they would care; of course if the situation were reversed they would support their police and soldiers and border officials in the fight against mass civilian invasions. I say civilian invasions; however, due to many of those who break into the EU having "lost" or burnt their passports and proof that they are who they say they are (a huge and expensive headache and challenge for all EU nations and their immigration officials) many of those seeking a new life in the West could be soldiers, former soldiers, or even the dreaded 'T word'—terrorists. (We ask to see documents for a very good reason, in order to ascertain who is dangerous, who is peaceful, who is useful and who is, for instance, a paedophile or a wife-killer.)

We know that drug, weapon and sex trafficking occur frequently within the large migrant communities who gather in large numbers at the weakest points of the EU border system (Bulgaria is not a wealthy nation, more EU funds will be needed to peacefully control the border, which means all EU citizens paying more tax in order to resolve the situation).

The conflicts on the EU's borders have been simmering for quite some time. Just prior to COVID, the escalation and flash points were located in Greece (on her border with Turkey); now there has been a noticeable shift towards the 'Balkan route' through Bulgaria/Romania; next it could be Italy once again. Word spreads from migrant camp to migrant camp. Workers for pro-immigrant NGOs (and anti-border political activists) tell migrants everything they need to know in order to breach national borders, providing written scripts and advice for their interactions with German immigration officials or French officials or British officials.

My research hasn't uncovered any of these (perhaps well-intentioned) 'handlers' providing any communiqués in Romanian or in Bulgarian. They assume the rock throwers amassed around the EU's borders are not in fear for their safety because none wish to live in Romania or Bulgaria (which Romanians and Bulgarians must consider to be born out of racism or xenophobia towards Romanians and Bulgarians by the people throwing rocks at them), so they don't help them to settle in those proud and strong EU democracies. They don't help them get every last penny they are entitled to by EU law and this convention and that and the other—all written by men and women who would refuse to guard any border on any condition because they are detached from the real world and from responsibility, which is why they lost the UK. Perhaps Bulgaria and Romania will be next, unless the Austrians and Dutch love and respect these nations. Time will tell if EU supremacy can be tempered enough to consider these relatively new EU states as close to being equals.

The situation makes for grim reading. Millions of people in the nations being frozen out of Schengen believed they would be true Europeans today, members of not only NATO and the EU but of Schengen also … and soon thereafter the euro—a "cure all" it is wildly hoped.

The depression, xenophobia, internal rifts and the lurch to the right the Austrian/Dutch decision on Schengen has caused within these Balkan nations is immeasurable.

After the strain and worry about the conflict in Ukraine (just next door), the hangover from COVID, and wearied and tested by the recession and high prices these nations were already at breaking point. I remind you of the Romania-annexation proposal (born out of fear), but there are other pacts and unions springing up, it seems, with each new passing day. There are talks of East Balkan Union this and West Balkans that; ambassadors are meeting ambassadors; deals and contracts are being signed and struck everywhere, all as a result of a lack of confidence in the EU and NATO's ability to ensure order, safety and peace.

It is for these reasons that the swift admission (May 2023 would suit) of these two nations into Schengen would create a strong sense of peace in Eastern Europe, reassurance for those who cry 'racism' or 'inequality' due to being kept out of the club, whilst simultaneously calming nationalist fears and keeping Eastern Europe within the EU and NATO.

There is no downside, so long as the EU no longer cites border security as justification for keeping Romania and Bulgaria out of Schengen.

If there were no rocks being thrown across EU borders by masked men without identity documents or proof of nationality, it seems that Romania and Bulgaria would today be in Schengen—if Austria and the Netherlands were being honest when they cited border security as the reason why the prospective nations were recently rejected by the Schengen union. So Bulgarians and Romanians are driven to think, *If these people hadn't illegally entered our territory, if they hadn't attacked us and forced us to defend ourselves, Austria and the Netherlands would have been shaking our hands today because we would be fellow Schengenites; it's all their fault, it's the fault of non-EU citizens!*

This, perhaps, is not the whole truth.

Schengen coming to Romania and Bulgaria (and Croatia) means companies from those nations will find it easier to compete against companies from Italy, Spain, France, Belgium, Germany, Poland, etc. Schengen is good for business, it allows a great deal of freedom and flexibility in terms of the movement of goods and people, yet there are many (companies/businessmen) in the West who dread the induction of two new nations into the long-running union within a union because (especially during recessions and times of high fuel prices) to compete against these new competitors, they know, will entail lowering the cost of goods, which will lower the wages or working hours of their workers, which will reduce their profits—which undoes their reason for being in business and engaging in capitalism in the first place.

Many benefit from keeping these EU nations out of Schengen, but if they are kept out for much longer they may no longer be EU nations. Schengen could easily become the straw that broke the EU's back because the EU barely weathered the storm of losing Britain and mishandling the pandemic as well as mishandling the conflict in Ukraine, so if Romania and Bulgaria exited the EU in this current climate most would consider this the beginning of the end for the EU experiment.

Chapter Twenty-Seven — Means Tested

Means tested—if you are born in the EU and refuse to work you will end up either homeless, living on the streets, or living in prison; however, if you can convince the liberal EU authorities that you are being persecuted in another country and offered protection and safe haven, how could the benevolent and loving EU ever allow you to become homeless?

Because to protect a "refugee" from Asia or Africa is not merely a case of allowing them to enter your borders; that is merely step one.

It is step two that interests non-Europeans and causes hundreds of millions to look towards Paris, Rome and Berlin for a new life, because step two is eternal welfare, free accommodation and privilege over the native working class.

Can you imagine twenty refugees that Berlin benevolently saved from Syria only to allow them to become homeless beggars on the streets of the capital a few weeks or years later? They gather together and hold placards complaining that Germany has taken away their free accommodation and their free welfare and free healthcare and free education and free clothes and free furniture and free smartphones.

There would be an international outcry, there would be leftist outrage with liberals everywhere crying, 'It is not enough to merely protect these people; we have to fund them and the lifestyles they choose until their dying day! Get them off the streets, now! Give them free accommodation, now!'

When ten German men are homeless, German elites look the other way and ignore their signs and complaints of social inequality; however, just because the homeless man is non-German born, his religion isn't native, and his culture isn't native, the German government would be accused of fascism and evil for not draining the treasury in order to make the foreigner's every dream and whim and desire become reality.

This is why many on the right feel justified when complaining about there being double standards in regards to the housing of refugees in their homeland, because the homeless native is eternally homeless until he does something to alter his situation, which is extremely hard to do without a great deal of intervention from third parties and charities. Yet when a refugee who has been granted refuge/asylum in the nation finds himself homeless and vulnerable, he will not remain that way for long, why? Because housing those in need in the EU is not means tested; rather, the native homeless are at the back of the queue for 'political reasons'. If they were not, how is it that every day in EU nations thousands of native poor citizens are evicted from their properties after they are repossessed by the bank? It is of course double standards to allow natives to end up living rough, homeless, whilst simultaneously housing every non-native migrant/refugee.

Free accommodation should be means tested in the EU; it would instantly end the housing of all non-native people in need because the native people most in need (those dying on the streets tonight in every European city, those who desperately require refuge) would of course be advanced to the front of the queue by caring and compassionate government officials, and if there was surplus housing remaining afterwards, once homelessness had been solved, then it could be allocated to others who were in need, yet natives must always come first, surely?

The situation in the EU at the present time is that the native homeless man and the refugee are not considered equal, but rather, the refugee is considered to be in more need and thus will not be allowed to live on the streets in the same way natives are allowed to be left on the streets whilst non-natives are given free accommodation, warmth and safety.

Chapter Twenty-Eight — 'I Need You, but I Hate You.'

Question—What am I?

I want to move from Asia/Africa to live in the EU, but I would never want to be buried in a cemetery if Christians or Jews were buried there or if homosexuals were buried there.

I do not like Jews, Christians or gays or liberals. I would absolutely hate to be forced to live in the next house to them for a multitude of reasons, yet I am desperately trying to get closer to them, even though I would rather they didn't exist.

I hate these groups of people, but I don't want them to ever leave Germany because these people are generous, even to people who viscerally hate them, like me.

I want the Christians and the lesbians and the beer drinkers and fornicators to remain exactly the same way because if they become like me they won't offer aid or free things or free apartments in Berlin.

I will accept their aid, their protection, their financial assistance, but I insist on developing my own nation within their nation, becoming a human cuckoo, laying my cultural egg in their nest.

I never want to become them or like them; I never want to change and also I never want them to change or to become like me because if these people were the same as me (the liberals, the Green Party/Christian Party voters, those racked by guilt who care deeply about the suffering of others and love others the way Jesus loved others) then I wouldn't be trying to get into the EU because the EU would look exactly the same as my homeland.

If Germans were like me, why would I want to live in Germany?

Answer—A very confused migrant/refugee who should be kept out of the EU at all costs.

Chapter Twenty-Nine — The Resettlement Lottery

In March 2023, the *Bild* newspaper in Germany published an internal confidential EU document that exposed the immense inequality in terms of sharing the burden of mass immigration and sheltering those who identify as refugees, with some EU nations accepting few to none whilst others (due to geographic location/politics) accept a disproportionately large number, which increases pressure on the state and taxpayers in every way imaginable.

Greece shelters 6.81% of migrants relative to her overall population; this figure is circa 350% higher than it should be according to the European Union's 'fair distribution' policy, which means Greece should be sheltering no more than 1.9% relative to her population.

Cyprus accepts 1.35% of all asylum seekers, yet they are expected to only induct/shelter 0.18%, for instance.

The inequality continues, with Germany accepting 35.42% of applicants despite her only being required by the EU to accept 22.05%.

Austria houses 4.85% of all asylum seekers, double what she is expected to accept as per EU rules. Her limit should be 2.46%.

The inequality works both ways, with the Netherlands being expected to accept 1.64% of the burden while only accepting and housing 0.64%—with the Netherlands preferring distribution to be based not on the population of the nation but on its economic strength, which is a good point.

Poland is an extreme example of the inequality and disparity in regards to sharing the migrant and refugee burden. She only shelters 0.86% while she should (according to the EU) be accepting more like 6.25% of asylum seekers.

This inequality only threatens to get worse with the Greek minister for migration and asylum, Panagiotis Mitarachi, stating in March 2023 that, 'In the first months of 2023, arrivals increased by 177 percent compared to the previous year, and if you look at the number of new migrants from January 2022 to January 2023, the situation is even more dramatic—the increase is 278%.'

The minister is currently begging the EU for 'comprehensive assistance' to tackle the problem of unwanted and harmful mass immigration.

How can the EU continue to exist in such an unequal form with some nations being hurt far more by the economic and social burden caused by mass immigration whilst others are more or less unscathed?

The EU is about conformity; the EU is about sharing experiences, which is where the Resettlement Lottery comes in....

***

The Resettlement Lottery is a revolutionary approach to handling mass applications for asylum/refuge in the EU (and elsewhere) and will ensure against wrongly admitting economic migrants or 'users' who are only purporting to be refugees, who are not driven by a desire to flee danger but by a desire to become rich and 'kept', who are driven by things like covetousness, idleness, greed and/or a desire to commit crime or terror attacks in Europe. Such individuals (if admitted) will only increase xenophobia against foreigners and will give genuine refugees a bad name.

The concept is simple; he who requests asylum within the EU shall be asked if he has a preference to be housed and protected in a certain EU nation more than another and why.

The nation allocated to the migrant/refugee will be chosen at random, the EU will not have direct input on a case-by-case basis. Once a nation's migrant/refugee quota of migrant/refugee numbers has been met (mandated by the EU), said nation will be removed from the Resettlement Lottery and will induct no new migrants/refugees whatsoever until, for instance, January 1st the following year when the Resettlement Lottery is reset.

It will be established that there is a preference in the majority of cases, which is suggestive that the individual is not afraid but wishes to benefit from the welfare, facilities and amenities and liberalism available in certain nations. For instance, the murder rate in certain Western European nations is higher than in Eastern European nations, so technically (in many ways) refugees would be safer living in Romania or Bulgaria than in France or Germany, especially when one considers that no terrorist attacks are likely to occur in Eastern European nations but are a regular occurrence in Western European nations due to mass immigration.

The applicant will next be asked if they still wish to claim asylum if it means becoming a part of the Resettlement Lottery, meaning that their new home nation within the EU shall be chosen for them at random.

If they answer, 'No,' (these questions can be automated as part of the Poly-interview process) it will mean only one thing—that they do not wish to relocate to the EU but, rather, only to certain places in the EU.

If they reject the EU deciding where they will be resettled, it will be assumed that the applicant is a racist, is a nationalist, hates certain EU peoples and nations or is not in fear in any way whatsoever and thus not a refugee or asylum seeker.

If the applicant agrees to the EU's Resettlement Lottery deciding which EU nation will feed, house and protect him in perpetuity, he will of course be deemed to be a genuine refugee, who is happy to be resettled anywhere, because safety is his first and last priority.

Why would liberal and tolerant German taxpayers be happy to fund the housing, education and healthcare and food bill for the foreign citizen who refuses to live in Poland because he doesn't like the Polish? Or who refuses to live in Bulgaria because they are not 'Western enough' for him? Such liberals should and would be outraged at this bias and favouritism.

Chapter Thirty — Billboards, Advertisements, Posters and PR

How can European politicians complain or be surprised about continuing unending waves of mass immigration when there are no billboards on the border or in Middle Eastern or African nations discouraging this practice?

The EU knows where the majority of migrants originate, so it is logical to place adverts in newspapers in those towns, cities and regions, to deliver leaflets to individual properties (word will soon spread) and to invest funds also in large billboards throughout the nations in question dispelling the myths that many migrants-to-be have come to believe from people smugglers and others who benefit from mass immigration.

If these campaigns existed outside the EU's borders, the numbers of migrants caught illegally entering the EU would decrease, this is certain. Yet if the will isn't there for such a bold approach, the EU reserves the right to erect large billboards all along the southern border of the EU facing those amassed on the other side, which would make it clear that 'there's no room at the inn'.

Examples of Billboards/Posters

This is Sayid (a photo of Sayid accompanies the text). Sayid was born in this town. He is a criminal; his family were forced to pay €60,000 to repatriate him to Iraq. Don't be like Sayid because Sayid is a criminal who destroyed his family rather than saving his family.

Crime does not pay. Invading the European Union does not pay.

Do not make Sayid's mistake. Work hard in your homeland, raise it up, choose honesty and hard work and your life will be blessed, or follow Sayid's example and next month it will be your face on this billboard....

***

In Germany, 262,000 people are homeless. Please turn around; we have no room for you.

In Britain, 271,000 people are homeless. Please turn around; we have no room for you.

In France, 300,000 people are homeless. Please turn around; we have no room for you.

In Spain, 29,000 people are homeless. Please turn around; we have no room for you.

In Italy, 51,000 people are homeless. Please turn around; we have no room for you.

(Figures accurate as of 2023 according to multiple homeless charities including Shelter as well as NGOs and government reports. The true figures are likely much higher.)

***

Millions are unemployed in Europe, so why are you coming?
Think before making the long journey for no reason....

***

Those who ignore such posters, leaflets and billboards will be saying, 'We know there are people suffering in your nations, we know that millions are unemployed, we know that there's a huge homeless problem in Europe and drug and alcohol abuse problem and crime and poverty and apathy and depression, but we do not care. We want to come regardless of all of your problems because we don't care about you, we only care about ourselves.'

The EU is not Heaven; this fact needs to be broadcast far and wide, only then will the migrant waves cease.

Chapter Thirty-One — Smuggler-Spies

(This chapter follows on from the chapter 'Taxes, Prison Sentences and Deterrents')

You would seek to repatriate the illegal (trespassing) immigrants as soon as humanly possible, as humanely possible, for a myriad of reasons, yet one shouldn't be as hasty when it comes to the repatriation of people smugglers and their proxies.

These individuals can be 'repurposed' in short order to become your eyes and ears within people, sex, drug and gun-smuggling rings, smashing the criminal gangs before a single illegal immigrant, bag of heroin, sex slave or automatic pistol is able to penetrate the EU's sieve-like borders.

The extra fees/penalties levied against the smugglers themselves and those who (knowingly) drive the cars and trucks that bring in all manner of illegal items and contraband every day, every week, every year are not about spite, hate or revenge. Rather, they exist in equal parts to demotivate (to prevent copy cats) and to motivate—to encourage them to switch sides.

Fact: Smugglers are non-ideological; they are driven by a desire to get rich quick. They desire neither to be imprisoned in the EU nor forced to beg their (already struggling) family members and extended family members and friends and neighbours and imam or priest to 'bail them out' due to the embarrassment and shame such a thing would surely induce, for most people at least.

Smugglers will have a choice. Phone fifty friends and neighbours begging for money, which they will be paying back for the remainder of their lives, or work for the EU for only thirty days before being fully released without payment of any kind being needed to be paid.

What will this achieve?

Paranoia and hysteria in the ranks of every criminal organisation currently profiting from people, drug, gun and sex-slave smuggling because the higher-ups in these organisations will never knew who has been caught, who is working for the EU, and thus will never know who they can and cannot trust. This means that regular infighting and demotivation will occur, with criminals likely executing other criminals who have nothing to do with the EU and are not smuggler-spies.

The smugglers who agree to the EU's terms will not be on the payroll, they will not receive benefits or a pension; rather, they will work for limited periods only (perhaps just thirty days) being motivated dually by 1/ the debt they owe to the EU, which would be transferred to their family and community and latterly on to themselves, being 'written off' in exchange for service and 2/ the fact that if they do not perform as expected, the EU will make it known that they are spies for the EU.

Such criminals, whose actions cause devastation far and wide throughout Europe, who choose this option will have no choice, absolutely no choice but to complete the tasks assigned to them by their EU handlers.

They will report on migrant movements on the other side of borders.

They will plant listening devices and tracking devices in properties and vehicles owned by criminal networks.

They will give forewarning to EU authorities of when smuggling operations will occur.

They will (in general) disrupt all smuggling operations and attempts to illegally enter the European Union.

Those who excel in this field can be retained for longer periods, yet their wages shall not be paid by EU taxpayers but rather will come from the profits of Poly-interviews.

Everyone wins, apart from criminals, liars, bullies and cheaters.

Before too long, it will be deemed too hazardous to attempt to smuggle anything through EU borders, which will cause those currently profiting from EU softness/weakness on the border to engage in other activities, hopefully honest and non-harmful activities, many, many miles away from the EU....

Chapter Thirty-Two — Why Many Middle-Class and Upper-Class Natives Hate Patriotism

There are, of course, many exceptions, especially historically, yet more and more of those who vote 'right' are from the 'bottom of the pyramid'.

Let me start this chapter by sharing something quite interesting.

The far right (aka, nationalists) are 99% working class—the same is true of those described as far right in all European nations as well as in the UK and USA, etc. (Such individuals are regularly given the monikers rednecks, knuckle-draggers, neo-Nazis, little Englanders and so on.)

The far left is 99% middle/elite class but would be elated if even just 10% of their number were workers born to workers born to workers born to workers because that would reduce the appearance of supremacy; yet, in reality, the vast majority of socialists and far leftists are well educated/middle class and come from privilege. Their hearts are often in the right place, but more often than not, they lack the real-world experience and perspective necessary in order to make informed decisions on important matters such as open borders or mass immigration, things that cripple, terrify, displace and thus anger the indigenous working class.

The British far right, as an example (remember, 99% working class), take to the streets, march, demonstrate and then beg the other classes to vote for what is commonly referred to as a 'far-right party.'

The native indigenous (nationalist) worker makes a compelling argument. His pitch to the middle and upper class members of his tribe is, however, always doomed to fail. Here's why:

The working-class native says:

'Immigrants are pushing up house prices. Poor and lower-working-class indigenous workers like me will never be able to get on the property ladder now—we must continue renting, which is just throwing money away and making others rich. And renting emasculates men like me, the men who the other classes always expect to die in Flanders or the Somme or Berlin or Normandy or wherever to maintain their lifestyles and to maintain the class system as it exists.'

The middle/upper-class native says:

'We own property, so you say immigrants are increasing the value of our possessions? Great! You say this will cause more renters and, I imagine, higher rents also? Double great—I will rent out my second and third homes to capitalise; I may even build an extension or convert the garage to accommodate more workers, aka those who will enrich me.

'Oh, and about that whole dying for us thing; if you love your country so much and claim to be a patriot, understand what this means:

'You love this system. It is, after all, the only one you've ever known.'

The working-class native says:

'Immigrant crime and imported terrorism will end if you vote for our party of choice. We will save all communities—not only the white working-class community.'

The middle/upper-class native says:

'We don't care what colour or religion our workers are, it's irrelevant to us. The same applies to the tenants of our properties or those who work for us directly or who mow our lawn, cook our meals or clean our houses.

'If you remove every Irishman, you will still remain on the bottom rung; move every Bangladeshi and other non-Brit? The same thing applies. So you see, it's pointless fighting, you've already lost.'

The working-class native says:

'It feels as though our community is being undermined and disenfranchised, this is screwing up our kids and sending us all to the doctors in need of antidepressants. We need your help, your votes … please…. Just imagine millions of non-natives suddenly departing our shores and us getting our country back, imagine how many jobs would be available then and how happy the members of the working class will become if they never have to worry about money or jobs again, are paid a decent and fair wage, are all able to afford to purchase a property and no longer are forced into crime and insurmountable debt…. Please help us; please stop voting for the parties that are hurting us.'

The middle/upper-class native says:

'Hang on a moment. If getting rid of immigrants makes you rich, where's *that* money coming from? Wait, that's not my money, is it? You are saying that, in order to save your community, my community will have to make some cutbacks and changes such as employing locals, no longer outsourcing work to the Third World, and paying workers a decent wage (not the bare minimum but enough to give a man dignity and the ability to grow and become something more)?

'The psychological harm being inflicted on your community currently may indeed cease entirely if we vote for your guy or simply change our ways, but will I still be able to have four luxury holidays abroad each year, upgrade my car whenever I'm bored of the one I've got and dine out whenever I desire?

'If I help you, I will surely be forced to thereafter lose some of what I have fought to attain or inherited. Unfortunately, my class-challenged friend, I will continue to put myself and my immediate family first. I am sorry about your situation, I truly am; perhaps strong alcohol or heroin could help?'

The working-class native says:

'If you won't listen, we will shout louder and organise … we'll march and scream and eventually you will be forced to help us. We feel scared, trapped, powerless and vulnerable. If we were each given £10M, we would likely move to your area or leave the country entirely, but we can't escape (to another class or country) because no one is handing out large checks to us unfortunately.

'We are so desperate now and so sick and tired of feeling low and beaten that we will really become a force to be reckoned with at the next election, just you wait and see!'

The middle/upper-class native says:

'Okay, okay; you've had your fun; you should've given up by now. But considering you just don't get it that the system has to remain the way it is, otherwise the wealth of the minority will decrease as the wealth (and thus power) of the majority increases, I will now tell everyone I know to avoid the "far-right" parties like the plague and to treat with extreme suspicion any parties who prioritise the poorest in society or the native population.

'Further, I will become active in politics. If I'm a teacher or educator, I will begin to fight back against working-class natives as they attempt to change their fate.

'The Holocaust ought to work, yes. I will tell anyone who considers helping the cause of the indigenous working class that we better expect another Holocaust because "it makes one a Nazi when he insists on having the same opportunities and respect within society as other members of their own race".

'Don't these Nazis realise that they come across as socialists? This is what I tell people I am, a democratic socialist who likes the working class to live in "working-class areas", or ghettos, many, many miles away.

'We must all make a concerted effort to disrupt the activities of those who speak of liberation or of reforming the status quo. These people must be smeared and attacked; any tactic can and must be employed against them, even scaremongering that World War Three is the only thing to be gained by listening to the indigenous majority.

'I will now join one of those "anti-fascist" groups and join the other middle and upper-class privileged natives as we collectively rain down bottles and bricks upon the heads of the native working class.…

'They think *they* are Britain? No, *I* am Britain. Britain is about standing on the neck of the weaker man. The monarchy should have been a hint to these so-called "freedom fighters" that power and money talk—and as they have neither, the native working class needs to shut the hell up … or else!

'I will start my "anti-racism" campaign immediately. I wonder how many knuckle-dragging nationalists will figure out the racism part of "anti-racism" in actual fact translates to "me" and the anti translates to "pro".

'Each time I shout, "Smash the fascists!" what I mean is, "I refuse to have my standard of living altered in any way by those I deem to be lesser than me."

'If only they had said they hated people richer than me … then perhaps, but only perhaps, I would join in their struggle as we would equally benefit and upward mobility would be felt equally by all.'

***

The working class desire a simple and quiet life and are not afraid to work hard in order to achieve this objective. They are essential to the other classes, without this class the other classes would starve, a fact that causes many non-working-class folk to develop a grudge against active workers. Such people will use mass immigration to 'punish' or to 'rub the right's nose in diversity' (see Lord Mandelson's comments regarding why he/the left imported as many immigrants as possible). When politicians say 'right', they mean the working class; they are bullying the little guy, picking on an easy target.

The inclusion of new workers from the four corners of the world in the second half of the twentieth century in the majority of capitalist democracies in the West is one of the greatest evils in history, not because those nations are 'too good' for foreigners but because of the intent: The ongoing conscious and subconscious effort to eliminate the need for a native working class, to transform this community into little more than impotent consumers.

This is not, as some have wrongly claimed, a coordinated effort by the left (and certain shady groups) to 'genocide the white race'. There is no concerted and agreed upon plan outside the isolated cases of the Mandelsons and Blairs of this world who use racial politics as a sort of therapy, giving the hard-working and strong underclass (feared by all elites) a bloody nose, setting a fire in his apartment but forgetting he and his family live upstairs.…

The greatest lie in history: The class system is natural, normal and healthy.

If you identify as working class, middle class, or upper class/elite class by virtue of birth/blood alone I would encourage you to think, just for a moment, about what you believe in—that you are agreeing to be defined and judged by the actions, achievements and possibly mistakes of your parents and grandparents because they were told they were a certain class and you (for some reason) inherit that class, so others will know your worth and eventual place within the community and who your friends will or won't be is already predetermined, as is your future employment or lack thereof.

***

The working class at the present time throughout Europe, the UK and elsewhere are browbeaten, lacking drive and motivation because the system is engineered to keep them where they are until they die. They subconsciously realise their grandchildren's grandchildren will inevitably be born into the same situation and will be equally depressed and lacking in confidence as themselves.

What the native working man envies the most is not money, nice cars, houses, jewellery or holidays to the Caribbean; no, he envies the confidence of the middle/elite classes and how at ease with life they seem—and this envy/jealousy more often than not mutates into resentment and eventually hate-filled anger.

The working man wants nothing more than for his children to respect him because he is able to provide for them, for his family to be safe, his wife fulfilled and to no longer have to walk the earth believing that they are (for some reason) genetically inferior to everyone who doesn't look and sound like them—inferior to middle/upper class natives.

He wants to save his children from his fate but can't; then he realises it's his fault that they are growing up in poverty because he chose to create them. This realisation is soul-crushing.

Then the blame-shifting begins in order for the man to remain sane, at least to some degree.

Endless moaning, recriminations, angst and anger follow as well as divorces, children taken into care or running away. Very few boys and girls living rough (if any) across the world in 2023 came from privilege or wealthy families. Those young people suffered so much; they were beaten down so much by society, the unnatural class structure, societal expectations and by the negative fallout/consequences of multiculturalism and a supressed working class that they felt their only option was to leave their community.

They left to avoid a fate long known to them—if they had remained, they would have taken their own lives, if not immediately then gradually via drug/alcohol abuse.

Homelessness is the only thing keeping them alive. They cannot return to their community, they were too damaged by it to even imagine giving up their newfound freedom—the freedom that comes from not identifying as or being a part of a particular class. This is how broken our societies are, this is how urgent the situation is; those cold and lonely souls deserve to be happy and they deserve unconditional love also. They are not working class; they are humans, native humans. Why are we fighting among ourselves?

Chapter Thirty-Three — The German Villas in Turkey

Turkey, its natural beauty, its uplifting climate (for those from Northern Europe, at least), its culture and its long and interesting history attract millions of tourists and hundreds of thousands of 'retirees' from across the world who choose to live in Turkey full time, or at least for six or nine months of each year.

Among this number are found Germans—many thousands of Germans.

***

Scenario:
Ten thousand German second-home owners in Turkey choose to leave their detached, high-end and modern Turkish villas on Christmas Eve because they all wish to spend Christmas Day in their homeland (where they own and maintain apartments or houses).

The ten thousand Germans will not return to their luxury villas in the exclusive and crime-free villa zones where they are located until June because in this scenario the ten thousand Germans spend six months living in Turkey and then six months living in Germany. Such arrangements and lifestyles are quite common.

It is Christmas Day in Germany. The German people and their representatives desire to feel happy, joyous, relaxed and calm; but instead their attention is drawn (by the media/special interests/big business/certain political activists/NGOs) to the seemingly coordinated riots and protests at flashpoints taking place along the EU's external borders.

When a German sees migrants trying to break into Greece or Bulgaria, he knows that what the migrant is actually doing is trying to break into Germany: Because once you have entered one EU country it is far easier to continue your journey into other EU countries, the heart of them all being Germany. Many non-EU citizens see the EU as 'belonging to Germany' more than her belonging to the Union (Germany being Russia and the EU being the USSR) due to the strength of German efficiency and consistent output. The problem is when you are successful, those who are not successful will attach themselves to you in an attempt to become successful themselves.

The ten thousand second-home-owning Germans watch on in shock as they witness pictures of women holding their crying children and babies, the scenes look totally foreign to modern Germans due to being untouched by tribalism, war and suffering, unlike their forebears between 1914 and 1945. Many Germans will cry when watching the footage of the migrants pleading to be let in, they feel bad because they have built an amazing civilisation and society and are capable of achieving the weighty feat of maintaining order and peace by remaining ever responsible, dutiful, hardworking, optimistic and active, taking life by the horns as if it were a bull, and then they think, *Why should I be so happy? Do I really deserve to be happy? And how can I be happy now that I know I could end the suffering of every refugee in the world simply by letting them all move to Germany?*

The ten thousand Germans become more and more depressed due to witnessing the suffering of refugees on the one day of the year (Christmas) they thought they could allow themselves to be happy and joyful, forgive themselves and their ancestors and look forward with strength but love also.

The ten thousand Germans are watching the same charity appeal on television that features the German and Turkish presidents standing together, smiling and shaking each other's hand. The German president explains on television that he is calling upon all Germans who own unoccupied second homes in Turkey to allow refugees to temporarily live there until a better solution can be arranged.

Within minutes of seeing the charity appeal on their screens, the majority of these ten thousand Germans dial the number on the screen and declare their willingness to help end the suffering that is causing to ruin their Christmas, but rather than offer their properties temporarily, they offer to gift their properties free of charge to those who (they know) would have been given free housing/accommodation in Germany if they were able to breach the border and enter illegally—in their mind, it made no difference whether they paid to help these people now or be forced to pay for them (via higher taxes) later.

The news soon reaches Turkey, both presidents celebrate, it is a Christmas miracle! Yet, when news reaches the group of migrants camped next to the EU border fence in Northern Turkey, the reaction (to being gifted expensive modern villas in exclusive resorts in Turkey) is the opposite of joyous as one journalist discovers after relaying the news to one of the recipients of this great gift from the Germans:

'So, what do you think about the Christmas gift that so many Germans have chosen to give to you?'

'We don't want to live in turkey, we hate it here.'

'Wait a moment, what is so wrong with Turkey? Millions travel to Turkey each year to enjoy holidays there, weekend breaks or even all-inclusive fortnight beach holidays, staying in villas or hotels, and no small number of expats have chosen to retire to Turkey also; are all of these people mad, in denial or masochists? Is Turkey really as bad as you are claiming it is?'

'*No, okay, Turkey is a nice place, but we want to live in Germany, in Berlin.*'

'Out of curiosity, do you plan to move to the Kreuzberg or Neukölln quarters of Berlin, for instance?'

'*Yes, yes, I have, family and friends from Syria and Turkey in Kreuzberg, this is where I want to go.*

'Did you know that the majority of residents in Kreuzberg are ethnic Turks and that Islam rather than Christianity is the dominant religion in Kreuzberg (just like in Turkey) and Arabic and Turkish are the dominant languages spoken in that part of Berlin (just like in Turkey)?'

'*Yes, so what?*'

'Don't you find it strange that you are willing to risk your life to escape from Turkey (to run away from Turks) but your destination (Germany) has millions of Turks, with most living in the areas where refugees and new economic migrants will surely be living? Where you want to live the view from your window will be the same as the view from a window in Ankara, the language your ears hear around you will be the same as the language you hear in Turkey, the culture all around you will in the migrant enclaves you wish to emigrate to be the same as the culture here that you are seeking to flee from. It will be as though you never left Turkey in the first place if you remain within the self-segregated Turkish quarters, so what's the point in you venturing from here to there? Help me understand why you are not happy about receiving a free villa in Turkey.'

'*I want to go to Germany because the EU is there and the EU is loving.*'

'I think you are confusing opportunism, taking advantage of desperate and scared migrants (future low-skilled workers), desiring to import the taxpayers who will sustain the indigenous middle-class and public servants through their very long retirements with "love".'

'*No, you are wrong; they are loving and they are generous.*'

'They demand that every citizen pays a multitude of taxes, which increase each and every year; this is generous?'

'*But they don't demand that I pay them taxes….*'

'Not yet they don't, but give it time. I wonder, would you stop throwing rocks at EU border guards and police officers and choose to remain living in Turkey if tonight, as if by magic, the entire population of Turkey was transferred to Germany and all Germans (and thus their culture, welfare system and productivity and work ethic) were transferred to Turkey?'

'*So, all Germans would be in Turkey and all Turks would be in Germany?*'

'Yes, the buildings and roads and infrastructure would remain the same, the only difference would be the people; what's your choice?'

'*I will stay here if the Germans come here.*'

'So I was right earlier then, when I said you didn't want to move to Germany?'

'No, I told you I am moving to Germany, I want to move to Germany.'

'I disagree because you would remain forever in Turkey if the German people resided in Turkey. That means that rather than wanting to move to Germany, what you are actually intending to do instead is to attach yourself to the Germans (the people, not the state) whether they reside in Central Europe, in Turkey or on Mars. If every German left Germany you would leave also, right?'

'Yes, I guess. But so what if I want the Germans to help me? They want to help me and they are very capable and hardworking people, they can easily build a few extra houses and spare a little food and healthcare. I am sick also, by the way.'

'I hope that, if you ever make it to the migrant enclaves of Berlin or other towns and cities in the EU, you do everything possible to integrate into the majority culture, learn the language as soon as possible and detach yourself from welfare when safe to do so because not to do these things will cause you to remain an eternal "outsider" or non-integrator, which is your right (because Germany has outlawed intolerance and hate speech/thoughts). However, due to you disclosing that it is the German people you wish to follow around and be close to, rather than Germany, if you don't become German in every way your relationship with this people will only be one-sided, them benefiting you. I know these people feel great sadness, shame and embarrassment due to their actions in World War I and World War II, but do you really believe they deserve to share the fruits of their labours with strangers from ten countries away who refuse to integrate or support themselves and who will continue following the German people around wherever they go?'

'Oh. I hadn't thought about it like that. Why would German people be happy that I am only there because they are there but I never ever want to be like them in any way? I want to remain Muslim and my culture will remain Syrian and I do not plan on speaking German because the Germans will pay for translators for me. I need to think about what you have said because you're right; the EU is not a physical place with physical borders, the EU is a people, the European people, and wherever they go, the same ideals and societies we see in Europe will go also. I am happy to say, "I am going to Germany," but it feels wrong when I say, "I am going to the Germans for help."

'I need to think about things because I know not all Germans are pro-immigration or pro-refugees, which means that when I am relying on Germans to keep and protect me, despite me not liking or loving them enough to integrate or replicate their culture, beliefs or traditions (the things that made them successful and strong enough to attract me to them I the first place), in reality I am relying on the German Government to continually convince all Germans to accept me and other refugees and migrants because I know that if the government vanished in a flash, every refugee and economic migrant would instantly choose to run away from the German people because only a tiny minority of Germans (who don't

live in the segregated immigrant areas) would be willing to share the fruits of their labour with millions of people. These few are self-hating and self-harming and guilt-ridden masochists. Most people are workers; few have the luxury of savings, second or third homes or a "job for life". Yes, I see it now, it is only certain politicians, factory owners and detached elites who are calling me to Berlin; most workers don't want a sudden influx of millions of new job and housing competitors, why would they?'

The ten thousand German villas are grudgingly accepted by the EU citizens-to-be, but none are used as a temporary or permanent place to seek refuge and shelter. Rather, almost all of them are quickly sold by the migrants within weeks of receiving them as gifts from the Germans and they use the money to pay people smugglers to transport them to Berlin....

Chapter Thirty-Four — Averting a Bulgexit and a Romexit

Might these two nations soon choose to open their borders in order to permit untold millions of non-EU citizens to enter Europe (knowing they will only use their nations as a land bridge to France, Germany and the UK) after their recent 'Schengen snub'?

What would you do if you had followed every rule, swallowed all of your pride, diligently defended the border against rock-throwing men from five countries away and dutifully bowed to EU bureaucracy and to the EU flag all in the interest of being accepted and treated as equals, and after all of that, the EU says, 'Not good enough' ? I believe many would be tempted to reverse course immediately and dramatically.

I believe both nations will keep the borders closed for now; however, if the embarrassment and criticism continues in regards to how these nations choose to defend themselves, this policy could soon change:

Monday: The Balkan nations are guarding the EU borders perfectly.

Tuesday: Masked men throw rocks and other objects at EU border guards.

Wednesday: Border guards attempt to defend themselves and the border.

Thursday: Romania and Bulgaria are 'banned from Schengen'.

Friday: Romania and Bulgaria open their borders and allow ten million human beings to pour into the EU, guaranteeing its demise due to there being finite resources and jobs and housing and schools and hospitals in Europe. Such an influx would kill the Union.

Saturday: The EU complains that Romania and Bulgaria are now being 'too friendly' to those who want to benefit from becoming EU citizens by giving them what they have been demanding for years: access to the land bridge to the EU known as Romania and Bulgaria. Few migrants or refugees choose to settle in those nations because they put the interests of their native people first.

If you attack nations for keeping people out, how long do you think it will be until they learn it is far easier to simply let them all in, perhaps by cover of night? This would:

1/ Pacify the political activists and those who have made immigration/refugee resettlement their cause.

2/ Mean they would no longer have rocks being thrown at their heads—attempted murder. The new EU citizens are committing attempted murder every day; they are not armed with rose petals and poetry.

3/ Get the EU 'off their backs'.

How can we prevent these nations from destroying the EU by allowing millions of foreigners without documents or ID of any kind to flow directly into Vienna, Berlin and Paris?

1/ Advance these nations into Schengen immediately.

2/ Allow the military to guard the border.

3/ Treat these nations as EU equals rather than as a source of cheap labour and exports.

The EU mistreated the UK; then the EU lost the UK.

The EU treats migrants and refugees very well indeed, which is why she is attracting many million more migrants and refugees.

The EU is mistreating Romania and Bulgaria (and Poland and Hungary) … what do you think will happen next?

If EU citizens are not all treated as equals, if EU nations are not all treated as equals, what's the point in the EU continuing to exist? If Bulgaria hadn't joined the EU, she would be able to guard her borders with her armed forces, ensuring (as it was during the Cold War) that not a single human being would be able to enter the territory of Bulgaria; yet, because she is a member of the EU, she is not allowed to use her greatest and most powerful resource, her military, to guard her nation and borders because that 'isn't very EU', which is why the migrant crisis exists—because of EU rules, liberalism and continued weakness and placing the interests of non-EU citizens first.

National elections were held in Bulgaria at the beginning of April, 2023. I read today that the expected third largest political party in Bulgaria is a 'far-right' political party, are you surprised? I am not.

This party, which has previously called for tougher actions on the southern EU border to end the migrant crisis, would have received far fewer votes had Bulgaria been granted ascension to Schengen a few months ago, and fewer still if the Western EU states treated Bulgaria and Romania with respect and friendship rather than using them as a scapegoat and an eternal victim of their 'mass immigration blame-shifting' as they continually take no responsibility for being the migrant/refugee lure.

Chapter Thirty-Five — What Would You Prefer?

What would you prefer, one million men standing up to tyranny and evil, leading to their emancipation, eternal happiness, independence and self-sufficiency, meaning their freedom and happiness will not cost you a thing, or for the one million men to abandon their homeland, rather than fight for it, and force their way into your homeland, at which time you will be forced to protect the million men (and their families), build houses for them, feed and clothe and educate the million men and their children and their wives and their mothers-in-law who all chose not to oppose tyranny or evil or privation or martyrdom but instead chose to recreate their culture and nation in their chosen host nation, your nation?

If you permit one million to come this year, two million will come next year whilst tyranny and evil spread in the countries they left and good people flee to relative safety in faraway places such as the EU and Britain (displacing natives) and in so doing cause xenophobia, mistrust, ghettoization and tribal rifts and culture clashes. Yes, many of those who arrive in the EU and Britain have suffered terribly in their pasts in various ways (as have many men and women in the West), yet their presence in the West is often divisive, especially during periods of high unemployment and mass native flight in combination with an increase in migrant crime, refugee crime and first and second-generation migrants engaging in acts of terrorism.

If the one million men arrive in Britain and EU nations and the USA with one million sons, will not the one million sons eventually return to their homeland in adulthood, when a full citizen of a Western state, when a soldier or sailor or marine, when sent by his adopted nation or host nation to finally defeat the tyranny that their fathers refused to fight against and defeat?

What father would prefer his son or grandson to die fighting the battles he chose to avoid?

Is it the case that the majority of self-identifying refugees intend to ban their sons from joining the armed forces of the Western state that saved them and sustains them in every conceivable way?

Yes. Of course these sons will be thoroughly discouraged by their self-segregating family and community from engaging in public service or volunteering to defend the nation because that was not the father's experience. Not wishing to feel shame or guilt or regret at his actions, he informs his son that, 'Only fools stand up to tyrants,' and 'Only fools defend the nation. It is better not to defend, it is better to wait until you have allowed your community and nation to deteriorate before slipping away silently in the night, leaving all your problems behind you as you break into the domains of other tribes, as you head to another land of liberal and tolerant people who are easily pushed around due to their collective guilt about empire, slavery, colonisation and excelling historically.'

Imagine a refugee arrives on Monday in England with his ten-year-old son and says, 'In only a few years, you will be old enough to join the British Army, my son. They will train you, strengthen you and improve you in every way in order to make you able and willing to defeat the tyranny I have just fled from. If and when the British people choose to intervene in our homeland directly, risking death, loss of resources and reputation and everything, you may die also, on the first day of the liberation, but at least I saved you when you were ten. However, I cannot save you in eight years' time, when you reach eighteen and are sent by Britain to liberate our ancestral homeland that I chose to abandon.'

What is the point in running if your sons and grandsons will return and fight and die in your place?

And if your blood doesn't return (because you ban your children from joining Western armed forces and propagandise their young hearts, filling them with hatred for those who saved you and feed you and protect you), and if only native Europeans venture to your homeland and shed blood to liberate your ancestral homeland from a tin pot dictator, how can you expect to remain in the Western states who gave you a passport and protection and accommodation and love? You cannot, the majority will politely request that you leave.

The problem with migration taking place during wartime is the natives are forced to tolerate the burden of refugees (the poorest are always hurt the most because elites and the middle class keep refugees out of their areas) whilst knowing those they are struggling to support (as taxes and rents rise and jobs and resources decrease) never desired to relocate to their nation (the host nation). The refugees believe their host nation inferior or only their second preference. They're only there due to circumstance, and if one nation said, 'No,' to every refugee of every race and religion and gender being resettled there, they would be forced to live in a different nation, more liberal or masochistic than the first. They would be happier living in the liberal and tolerant area, which is why refugees should be housed in the most expensive and sought-after areas of London and Paris and Berlin and Rome as, if multiculturalism is a gift, the elites will welcome that gift with open arms surely? Refugees don't wish to live next to the unemployed nationalistic working-class natives who desire a vote on immigration and better control of their borders.

Why did Britain win the Battle of Britain against formidable Germany? One word: duty.

Britons smiled every day after surviving another bombing raid. Only the children were sent to the countryside; all men and women including the young and very old stood their ground and prepared for absolute oblivion! This is how you win, this is how you maintain the homogeny and continuity of nation and people and culture—duty and purpose and courage and incredible individual power.

All must fight, none should ever flee; none should ever surrender. If you do, you should leave your culture and language and religion and world outlook and ego behind in the nation you abandoned when you impose yourself upon the British and French and Americans who have a long track record of standing up to tyranny even if it costs millions of lives and rivers of native blood.

No one wanted to storm the Bastille, those epic heroes each expected to die, yet that dark place needed to be stormed, and by the sacrifice of those supermen and superwomen France is today a republic; which is why foreign cultures and gangs and self-segregating communities in that nation should integrate or leave immediately. Enough is enough.

Chapter Thirty-Six — Have You Ever Been Happy, and Do You Know What Awaits You?

How many migrants/refugees are contrarians, cynics and pessimists in general? Will they ever be happy? Can they ever be made happy or pleased so long as people give them what they want and demand, rather than what they need?

How many migrants/refugees are reckless, impatient, non-conformist, undisciplined and dangerously impulsive (creating babies, dependants, in refugee camps when they are dependants themselves, for instance), who 'live for today' (YOLO) in general? Will they ever be happy? Can they ever be made happy or pleased? (Was it more their pre-existing condition that put them on the EU's borders rather than a change in circumstances?)

The homeless population of the United Kingdom stands at a staggering, embarrassing and shameful 300,000 people, as of April 2023; the numbers are not much better in EU nations. (Homelessness dramatically rose whilst the UK was a member of the EU. It is hoped that this number will now fall, due to there being fewer job competitors from EU nations able to so freely compete against the native working class after the Brexit victory.)

If 300,000 middle-class Brits camped out on the edge of the EU's border fence with Turkey on the Greek or Bulgarian side, demanding entry, throwing rocks, and displaying the fact that they had babies, Turkey would likely not desire these people to enter. Yet, due to them being able to present documents, ID and their degree certificates and curriculum vitae, they would likely be admitted, once Turkey noted that these individuals would likely benefit the Turkish nation due to them being able to prove instantly that they had been patient in the past, they had had to 'defer happiness' in the past (higher education/apprenticing/starting at the bottom/becoming homeowners, etc.) and that they could be disciplined, that they were not reckless by nature and (given the right conditions) would thrive, thrive, thrive due to being able to prove that they were not contrarians (rather conformists) and that they must be optimists to have been able to complete higher education (to stay the course) and to have excelled in the workplace, been promoted, etc., and purchased property.

If, however, the 300,000 Brits camped out on the edge of the EU's border fence with Turkey on the Greek or Bulgarian side demanding entry were throwing rocks, displaying the fact that they had babies and were all yesterday homeless in the UK (the entire homeless population of the UK who were choosing to 'try to get a better life' in Turkey), Turkey would certainly not desire these people to enter for a multitude of reasons, including them likely not having many supporting documents, degree certificates or curriculum vitae. Turkey would ask this group why it was that the majority of the tribe remained in their homeland rather than fleeing, to which there could be no reply other than, 'I am a refugee, I have a baby, you must help me!'

Turkey would say no to those who had a long history of problems in their homelands, including extended periods of homelessness, in exactly the same way as the majority of Brits would turn away a homeless man or woman who knocked on their door asking for safety and sanctuary within their home, with their family.

***

There are many people in England, France, Germany, Portugal, Hungary, Italy and elsewhere throughout Europe who have been diagnosed with paranoid schizophrenia and delusions of persecution who often report having an (irrational) fear of persecution. Many others have delusions. How many at the border today who claim they are persecuted and terrified are this same way, their condition worsened and aggravated by PTSD and change?

Those who are living on the EU border (who desire entry into the EU ASAP) claiming they are afraid for their lives may be telling the truth, in the same way the New Yorker tells the truth when held in a secure psychiatric unit as he claims the government or aliens are seeking to harm him or persecute him or kill him. And the extreme circumstances that led many Asian and African men and women to make the trek to the EU border (war, famine, misogyny, racism, tribalism, disease, criminality, rape, domestic abuse, religious conflict, racial conflict) would only contribute to a worsening of mental health, paranoia and delusions rather than cure or assuage these things.

Are they lying when they say they are in fear for their lives? No.

Will they be raped or robbed or killed if they return to their homelands? Maybe.

Will they be raped or robbed or killed if they force their way into the EU or are invited in? Maybe.

It is an illusion and fantasy that being present with the borders of the EU automatically makes a person invulnerable to rape, bullying, persecution or mental illness, an absolute fantasy.

Rape is common in the West. Most rapes are not reported, most rapists are never imprisoned. There is no death sentence for rape, unlike in many non-EU nations.

There are more muggings in the West—petty and violent crime is widespread, few venture out into towns and cities after dark, unless in large numbers.

There's more sports-related violence—this will be a culture shock to non-citizens as they see tribal conflicts erupt out of nothingness over a game of football.

More alcohol-related violence—every few minutes in Europe someone is arrested for alcohol-fuelled crime and violence, an absolute non-occurrence in Muslim nations where alcohol is hard to find.

More racism and sectarianism—of every kind, of every type, of every variety, with Hindu communities having friction with Sikh communities, with Sikh communities having friction with Muslim communities, with native working-class Christian communities having friction with West Indian communities.

Those amassing on the borders of Europe should ask themselves why it was that the grandparents of former Prime Minister Boris Johnson found it necessary in the twentieth century (not very long ago) to change their name from the Muslim Turkish Kemal to the British/ European 'Johnson'. They should also wonder why the British royal family (also in the twentieth century) felt it necessary to change their surname from Saxe-Coburg to the more 'English sounding' and absolutely fictitious 'Windsor'.

The Kemals and Saxe-Coburgs didn't believe Europe was a bastion of tolerance and acceptance and love and brotherhood; they cast away their old selves in order to survive, they integrated and thus prospered. Yet many, perhaps a majority of those camped out on the EU's borders, have no interest in integration because they are not applying the correct way, they are not following the rules, they are attempting to make the rules, they are demanding entrance, which suggests they will never change their names or religions or cultures or personalities, which will guarantee generational friction and conflict. They are dooming their children and grandchildren.

And a lingering question remains. Why would a person only throw rocks once, at Bulgarian police officers? Why wouldn't that same person throw rocks once inside Germany or England or France or Italy if they once again became displeased and frustrated?

Chapter Thirty-Seven — Charity, Guilt-Tripping and Fascism — the Facilitators of EU Mass Immigration

Politicians are dependent on voters, yet they gaslight them into believing they are bosses (rather than public servants), which is why EU politicians sympathise with mass refugee immigration due to the majority of those arriving in the era of welfare (who would not come if welfare ended) destined to be wholly dependent upon taxpayers for everything for the remainder of their lives: The welfare migrant and pro-mass immigration career politician are the same person; they put their own needs first and the needs of taxpayers and providers second.

Both groups' success (of facilitating mass immigration in tandem with mass migrant welfare dependency) relies on one of three things—charity, guilt-tripping or anti-democracy measures (fascism).

Charity

Who are kinder, men or women? Sexists will, of course, without thinking, reply, 'Women, of course.'

(There is a misconception in regards to what denotes kindness, goodness and charity, with many "kind acts" not being kind at all but rather selfish acts, and often foolish self-harming acts.)

Is the husband who kills his family's pig less kind than his wife who only cooks the resulting pork chops in her electric oven?

If the wife eats meat but wouldn't kill an animal, it does not automatically mean she is kind, loving and one who should necessarily be making decisions for the household and the community; it simply means she is a hypocrite and in denial about how the real world works. It is not a sweet and innocent princess dream world where everything is pink and frilly, it is hard and visceral and dangerous for those unwilling to be independent and free, which means self-sufficiency and making tough choices even if they make you feel sad or guilty or the 'bad guy'.

In this scenario, the husband wanted to kill the pig far less than his wife because he had spent more time with the animal and, due to his nature being one of a shepherd, protector and leader he becomes torn between whether or not he will complete the deed he has dreaded for hundreds of days. He even thinks about exchanging his pig for a pig bred by and raised by one of his neighbours, but he stops himself from doing this, telling himself, *My wife would be destroyed if she were tasked with providing our family food by slaughtering the pig and my young child would be similarly psychologically harmed because they were birthed in a time of systems and business and classes, creating seemingly comfortable 'in-denial' existences for one and all—aided of course by prescription and non-prescription drugs and alcohol and holidays and endless toxic credit. It is because I wish to protect my wife and my child that I have chosen to take sole responsibility for providing meat to my family. I could ask my neighbour to do my difficult task for me, but how would that bring me happiness? If I cannot complete this task, I don't deserve a family and soon people will begin calling me weak, a user, or a parasite—and I am none of these things, for I am a man.*

The man exhibited great kindness to the pig in life; he then exhibited great kindness (and courage and strength) when he chose to sacrifice his own feelings by slaughtering the pig himself, rather than outsource that responsibility to another man somewhere else.

Yet, when he tells the foreigner that he doesn't have enough spare food and resources to share with him, his wife comes running out of the kitchen, scolding him for being a cruel and unkind fascist, and immediately invites in the man who calls himself a refugee as she tells her husband he must now breed more pigs in order to feed this new addition to the community.

Sometimes, as hard as it may be to understand at the time, the kinder person is the one who seems cruel and lacking in empathy and love. Children think responsible parents cruel when they impose curfews or insist that they don't drink alcohol or smoke cigarettes or consume recreational drugs, for instance.

Tough love and forward-thinking empathy outweigh momentary kindness (seeking to improve the mood of the help-giver just in that moment) every time. The man wants his family to survive, which is why he lives with the pig's death for many months before carrying out the slaughter. He does not want to do this thing; he needs to do this thing. He suffers a great deal well in advance of the slaughter knowing that it will all be worth it for his family when he is able to provide food for them to last the winter. He would feel equally pained for deciding to help refugees and economic migrants who asked him to share the family's pig with them. He/she who looks forward and thinks of tomorrow and the repercussions of every action will always appear cruel. He/she who never thinks about the future, who only thinks of today and their emotions, will always appear kind. Strength is kindness. Ensuring your family and community are perfectly cared for before helping others is kindness. Giving away everything you have and allowing balkanisation and ghettoisation to occur all around you is societal suicide.

Things Nice People Say and Things Bad People Say

The nice people say, 'Let everyone in (no borders). If things go well, if the huge and sudden demographic shift doesn't cause a surge in nationalism everywhere, tribalism and segregation everywhere, white flight everywhere, xenophobia everywhere, then everything will have worked out for the best—and I'm sure we will never end up like the indigenous peoples of South and North America whose friendly and warm welcome was rewarded with slavery and domination.'

The bad people say, 'Don't let anyone in until none of us in this tribe are homeless, none of us are unemployed, until we are free of self-harm and depression, until all streets are safe at all times in every land—because why shouldn't they be safe? Why do we tolerate disorder and apathy?'

Who is nice? What is nice? Who is bad? What is bad?

Guilt-Tripping

Radical political activists use guilt-tripping tactics as a means to break down a person's instinctual resistance to sharing the fruits of their labours with non-citizens from faraway lands—despite many natives being poor and underprivileged.

The principal targets of these guilt-tripping attacks are women, due to female compassion, female empathy and the suggestion that all women are or should be 'motherly'. All girls are given baby dolls to 'look after and nurture' when they can barely walk or talk. This crafts their nature; this makes them perfect targets for these shrewd political operators who know exactly what the end result of their reporting on the migrant crisis will be.

When the target is bombarded with imagery of non-citizens in an unhappy state, she is no longer a woman. In that moment, until she opens her purse, she becomes a little girl again as she imagines the non-citizens to all be dolls and teddy bears that only she can 'rescue'. She is not thinking about the future state of the economy of her homeland or the multiple languages that will soon be spoken in her child's school, which can in no way improve the education of her child; it can only cause to hinder it.

The pro-open borders radicals know that women in particular (but also a large number of irresponsible men also) will desire to 'go back in time' to the point directly before they viewed the harrowing photos of the migrants suffering on their journey to life in one of the big EU mega-cities after witnessing the footage so selectively shot. The radical activists know full well that it will become the driving force behind 'motherly' and guilt-ridden middle-class European women sending the fruits of their labours to non-Europeans, believing that they are helping rather than being the cause of racism, ghettoisation and balkanisation throughout Europe, higher taxes, native flight, apathy, depression, self-harm and cultural oblivion.

In this case, such women are being specifically targeted, the result being known well in advance. This is cynical at best, a case of mass bullying, gaslighting and psychological manipulation at worst and many are complicit in the numerous 'sympathy campaigns' that unite business with activists and politicians and media. It's quite the circus.

The irony is if every European agreed with the pro-immigration lobby and demanded open borders, the former pro-immigration beneficiaries of high taxation and the big state would almost immediately become hyper-racist and hyper-nationalist. Why? Because they are happy to have some of the Third World, but they do not want all of the Third World, which is why they don't live near migrant enclaves, which is why they are married to a white Christian, which is why every one of their friends is white and why they would rather die than live in Yemen, Syria, Somalia or Angola, even in peace time when the sun is shining, because the person who shouts, 'African and Asian refugees welcome!' knows there is a 0% chance they will be moving in next door to them. 'We love refugees,' translated means, 'We hate the indigenous people and indigenous culture and we want to change everything.'

Anti-Democracy Measures/Fascism

Not asking the native people whether or not they are happy to house/pay for foreigners to be provided for, perhaps forever, within their society and culture even if it means native flight occurs and the need for reservations for the indigenous (displaced) poor = fascism.

The question 'Do you want there to be mass immigration?' can't be asked because the answer is, of course, obvious: No. The answer will always be a resounding no. Ask Somalians this question, Kenyans, Indians, Jamaicans, Koreans, Japanese, Russians, Germans, Swiss—the answer will always be the same. No.

One neighbour competes with another in a multitude of ways (quality of house, car, wife, possessions, wealth, rank, the redness of his roses, achievements, etc.). So it follows that he will certainly seek to compete against any newcomer equally as aggressively if not more so, due to him having everything in common with his native neighbour and almost nothing in common with the man literally from the other side of our planet.

A question must now be asked. If this competitive man supports immigrants moving to his neighbourhood, doesn't that mean he is deceiving them when he says he loves them and is desperate to help them? Surely he will continue his modus operandi of supremacy, peacocking, showing-off and self-aggrandising once there are immigrants and refugees in his street, his workplace and his daughter's school? If he treats the new people kindly but his native neighbour meanly, what does that make him, a self-hating racist?

Chapter Thirty-Eight — Epigenetics and the Mental Health Fallout of Migration for Migrants and Natives

Moving house is one the most stressful events in a person's life, for a multitude of reasons. Moving house is bad enough, but imagine if you don't yet have the second property secured, imagine you are waiting on the periphery of the EU's or the USA's borders—the anxiety, fear and tension (caused by moving house) is massively amplified.

Most who move city to city or town to village within their homeland often complain about the experience, yet they are rarely motivated to relocate by violence, war and conflict and would never say they are afraid they will come to harm during the relocation—things refugees have to contend with in addition to the regular psychological fallout caused by the house move.

Refugee camps are dangerous places because apathy, depression, desperation, hate, anxiety, fear and frustration fester and dwell there. Refugees are far more afraid of one another than they are of foreign police officers or border guards. Refugee-on-refugee rape, violence, intimidation, exploitation and abuse of every kind is the greatest cause of suffering to refugees. The examples are too many to cite, with this growing problem (*belligerent migration) on the borders of many nations and unions only seeming to benefit those who are ruthless and hard enough (or lacking sufficient empathy) to exploit the weak, desperate and vulnerable.

*I use the term belligerent migration after comparing the modern migration tactics we observe in 2023 compared with historical migrations. For instance, if the first European settlers in North America had demanded entry (or else), demanded free housing, protection and healthcare and rights of every kind including the right to vote as they wore balaclavas and hurled large rocks at the faces of the native chiefs and their sons and daughters, the country known as the USA would not exist in 2023 because the indigenous peoples of North America would have reacted to such belligerency and pressure with the tomahawk.

The Europeans may have argued, 'But we have suffered in the past, we can't (we don't want to) go back. You must forgive our rock throwing and our insistence that you should keep us and protect us and provide for us in every way because although we have just run away from one nation, it does not mean we will run away from this new nation. If the going gets tough, we will make our final stand here with you as soon as you embrace multiculturalism and liberal tolerance and change.'

The indigenous North Americans would have empathised with the belligerent foreigners, they may have truly desired to offer temporary assistance to them, but it would have been clear that the rock throwing and the massing at the borders and the thousands of separate incursions into the territory by groups of foreigners both small and large meant only one thing—that the newcomers would never integrate. They would never conform, would reject the tepee and erect houses instead, which they would guard with rifles and the Bible and then nuclear weapons, whilst the native culture and faith and blood were walled up in reservations far away.

An interesting Finnish study into the negative mental health effects of migrating during wartime (the study focused upon WWII in Finland) suggests that not only do incoming refugees/economic migrants develop mental illnesses serious enough to cause hospitalisation as a result of migration (those who remained in Finland during the war were found to have fewer mental illnesses) but also the native refugees who flee (native flight) upon being surrounded by waves of mass immigration will certainly also.

Applying the findings of the large and comprehensive Finnish study we see that, similarly, the native population becomes sufficiently changed via epigenetics to cause not only depression and self-harm (suicide is the leading cause of death in the UK for native men under the age of 50), but also it is the certain cause of increased self-medication via alcohol and drugs and a myriad of other self-destructive means to soothe those who have been displaced by incoming refugees and economic migrants.

We observe the same mental illnesses and alcoholism and drug abuse in Australian indigenous communities as we observe in Native American indigenous communities, as we also observe in indigenous British communities that have fled from mass immigration and refugees to enclaves in Northern England.

It is a serious problem ignored by most, a problem that is fuelling the rise in mass native suicide, increasing domestic violence and increasing crime and depression and apathy. This explains why Brexit occurred; what the uneducated call xenophobia and prejudice is in actuality the natural knowingness that epigenetics will cause mental illness and malaise and nihilism upon the occasion the majority suddenly become a displaced minority—as in the case of the native Australians, the Native Americans and the native British working class.

I would recommend all who have an interest in epigenetics and who desire to reduce mental illness in all communities, especially the native poor communities and the foreign communities that continue the practice of inbreeding, which is fraught with danger (this is another leading cause of a spike in avoidable mental illnesses springing up in the West), to read the Finnish study in question. It is independent and has nothing to do with immigration or refugees but everything to do with human beings and facts. If you ignore facts and epigenetics and science, it can only mean that you don't care about people, or at least it means you don't care about poor natives.

The Finnish study in question was led by Matti Pirinen from the University of Helsinki, Finland, who, along with his colleagues, looked at the genomes of circa 18,500 people to study how the genetic composition of ten populations across twelve geographic regions covering most of Finland changed between 1923 and 1987.

The study has been covered within the *New Scientist*, Newsweek and other mainstream publications, with the Newsweek article titled, 'Children of World War II Evacuees Were Hospitalized for Mental Illnesses Passed Down From Traumatized Parents' and the article in the *New Scientist* titled 'Effects of Finnish evacuation during second world war visible in DNA'.

I cover the interesting topic of epigenetics in greater depth in the companion work to this book, *The Sudden and Unexpected Multiculturalisation of Mayfair, Kensington and Belgravia, Which Ended Mass Immigration and White Flight in the UK.*

Chapter Thirty-Nine — Does Europe Need to Change to Suit Non-Europeans?

The 'softie-softie' approach at the border wildly misrepresents the true nature of EU nations and individual Europeans. Europe is a place where bullfighting is accepted as a cultural norm (and protected by the benevolent and peace-loving men in suits in Brussels). I remind EU representatives and politicians that whereas you may seek to give money to a person solely due to the fact that they have encountered misfortune and been hurt and lost, a sizeable portion of your citizenry feel the opposite way, for instance the many millions of Europeans who habitually watch or engage in blood sports involving animals or who participate in or enjoy watching boxing, mixed martial arts and similar violent and bloody pursuits that often result in injuries, brain damage and even death. Europeans, like their ancestors in the coliseum, watch such spectacles explicitly for the reason of hoping one or both men become terribly injured, bloodied or maimed; the audience in 2023 will boo the fighters if they don't throw enough punches at one another.

The EU audience has not changed since the times of the coliseums; Europe is still the lions' den, so does that mean these new refugee/economic migrant inductees are lambs to the slaughter?

Spain knows that the refugee will be terrified and startled to see dozens of bulls being forced to run through the town where they have been given accommodation and "safe haven" by the EU. It will seem foreign, chaotic, perhaps even barbaric to some who are more sensitive or who have experienced extreme trauma previously and been exposed to violence.

Spain needs to make a choice, as do all European nations—change everything to make Europe suitable for non-Europeans or remain the same, which requires urgent integration into the local culture, economy and gene pool (or, at the very least, a respect for all the individual nationalities and cultures and faiths present within Europe).

So the answer is no, Europe does not need to change; those who seek to be saved and protected by Europe need to change because Europeans are not forcing them to move to Europe. In fact, the vast majority of Europeans desire a zero percent rate of immigration to exist, just as Syrians do, just as the Sudanese do, just as the Chinese do, just as the Japanese do, just as everyone does, other than the few (such as big business) who benefit from immigration.

Chapter Forty — The Convenience of Diet Pills, Packets of Crisps and the EU

Mass immigration and millions seeking to leave their homelands at the start of the twenty-first century in search of a new and easier life in the EU speaks to the worst aspects of hypercapitalism and convenience. I see no difference between diet pills, processed ready meals, packets of crisps and clambering over an EU border fence—they all achieve the same end goal: making life easier, making everything more convenient and simple for the consumer in the short term, whilst causing to create dependency and irresponsibility in the long term, stripping us all of our power and purpose.

If you rely on diet pills rather than willpower and hard work to lose weight in order to improve your physical and psychological health, you will have learnt nothing; you will be dependent on pills for the remainder of your life as you choose to falsely believe you will forever remain weak, undisciplined, impulsive and unable to maintain self-control for any worthwhile period of time.

It is hard work to plant, grow, harvest, prepare and cook potatoes, which is why there are those who advertise already grown, already prepared and already cooked potatoes, which have been processed and placed into super-convenient packets stating, 'Life is hard, your time is important so don't waste it toiling and making food for yourself, let us do all the hard work for you. We have even added salt and oils and exotic flavours because you're worth it. Don't rely on yourself; rely on us. Buy our product and then you will be happy.'

The pitch to hard-working independent men and women everywhere from those who sell unnecessary products in order to make a quick profit whilst spreading demotivation and dependency and addiction and obesity is little different from the pitch the EU and pro-mass immigration advocates project to non-EU citizens far and wide.

The EU will not say, 'Come here and rely on us because you cannot cope on your own. Don't bother growing potatoes because as an EU citizen you will be entitled to welfare/benefit payments, which you can use to purchase processed foods such as packets of crisps from supermarkets in the EU. Become a dependent consumer rather than a free, independent man....'

They do not say this, yet when we observe EU leaders/bureaucrats in public, in meetings or at press conferences, their demeanour, their happiness, the way they seem to walk on air as if the EU is Heaven (for them it is) is just one of the ways that mega union blows the dog whistle to every free and independent man and woman on the planet to abandon their plough, to forget about building a house themselves, to turn their backs on tradition, self-sufficiency and strength and to do everything possible to make it to the EU, to make it to Heaven, where everything is so much easier and convenient, just like a packet of crisps (potato chips) or a diet pill.

The end result is obvious: Native dissatisfaction and native flight in tandem with the ruination of the independence and free spirit of every incoming migrant.

Where are the advertisement posters stating, 'Come to Europe and be a proud farmer'? They are nowhere because farming is 'someone else's' job or responsibility, because farming is hard work, and because farming is dirty and wet and sweaty and not at all in keeping with the tastes and appetites and etiquette of Brussels and the European Parliament who see themselves as being above these things. This is the crux of the problem.

We need to see Ursula von der Leyen looking stoic for a change, looking sad and browbeaten for a change, looking as though she works for a living rather than merely relaxing for a living whilst being financially enriched by EU taxpayers. This would be a great start; this would amount to a fair representation of all EU citizens rather than merely projecting the mindset and the condition of the select privileged few at the top. Such unpopular representatives need to realise that the EU is not about them, that no one cares what they look like or how wide their smiles are or how they are dressed, because EU citizens, like all citizens, expect and demand results. Smile and pat yourself on the back when you have achieved something, ending EU homelessness and the migrant crisis would be a good place to start.

It comes to something when a non-EU citizen not on the EU payroll (like me) finds it necessary to bail out EU leaders. If you want your snouts to remain in the trough, you need to work harder, much, much, much harder, and you also need to forget the nonsense idea of turning the entirety of the European continent into one huge concrete mega-city where nothing is grown, nothing is produced, where everything is clean and perfect and where every human being is unable to survive without being 100% dependent on the EU. This ambition will destroy you all.

Stop running away from responsibilities and stop infusing your egos and hubris into politics as there is no room for them. This is not about you; only the people matter, the people who have been present in Europe for untold thousands of years. They deserve much better. Either work harder for them and put them first or retire. Europe should not be remade in your image.

Chapter Forty-One — Two Important Questions; Two Very Different Answers…

Question One

Are you happy for ten million impoverished and underprivileged Arab or Sub-Saharan Muslims from Africa and Asia, who possess EU membership, to urgently relocate to European nation states where they will be housed, educated, protected, given healthcare, voting rights, passports and equal status even if they choose to self-segregate and balkanise and create culture clashes?

Question Two

Are you happy for ten million impoverished and underprivileged white Europeans to travel by dinghies and small boats across the Mediterranean to start a new life in an African country, which will be forced to accept them, integrate them, build houses for them, educate their children, provide translators for them, feed them, protect them and respect their wishes when they choose to create ghettos and when they create multiple subcultures and march and protest when they don't believe they are being loved as much as the natives or when they don't believe they are being granted enough land, property, wealth or power for no reason other than they were able to make it across the Mediterranean in dinghies or small boats and regularly march and protest against the perceived Europhobia they experience on a daily basis?

Many people who claim to believe in "EU principles" would likely answer yes to the first question but no to the second.

Yes, the figure of ten million is high, I am sure liberally minded and pro-high-taxation citizens would have preferred it if the figure were lower, yet the reality created by capitalism, medicine and internationalism is that we could easily come to see ten million Europeans seeking sanctuary in the future and equally as easily see ten or twenty million Africans and Asians choosing the option of resettling as a refugee in the West—often from many, many nations away.

***

Objections to poor Europeans (of which there are tens of millions) relocating to African nations from pro-EU liberals and big city elites:

'It is not fair on the native poor and working class of the African nation to import millions of foreign European job competitors.'

'The millions of Europeans would be 100% dependent on the African state, which would deplete local resources and funds, empty hospitals of medicine, empty supermarkets of produce and empty the treasury of money, necessitating dangerous borrowing of millions and then billions.'

'The sudden infusion of millions of foreigners into an African nation would cause fear to rise and then the phenomenon of "black flight" to occur as the European refugees and European economic migrants chose to form ghettos, creating German towns and English towns and Slovenian towns in the vein of Chinatowns all over the African nation, which would by now have transformed against its will into a multicultural and multiracial nation, with shop fronts and businesses in all European ghettos in the African nation displaying European languages and culture, rather than the native African language and culture. The Europeans would act in a racist and divisive way, certain to antagonise the native Africans who wouldn't wish to hear foreign languages or read foreign writing in their ancient homelands and sacred towns and villages—why would they?'

Why mass immigration and multiculturalism (presented as "benevolence" and "altruism") exist in the EU, which will certainly result in millions more refugees and economic migrants entering European nation states against the will of the majority:

Liberals want poor foreigners to come to Europe to work for them because they refuse to pay fair wages to the indigenous working class, who in many European nations won improved pay and conditions (via sacrifice, unions and epic commitment). If the unions had not safeguarded European workers, no European nation would be multicultural today; there would be no Turkish or Moroccan or Bangladeshi or Pakistani or Somali enclaves within European towns and cities. The success of the unions caused the greedy few to cast their gaze abroad instead, in search of new workers and new consumers who could be better controlled, or so they hoped and optimistically imagined. They were blinded by the potential profit so threw caution to the wind....

The native working class of European nations and Britain have been battered by liberals and elites for decades because they dared stand up for themselves. This is why white flight exists.

Importing Refugees Is Importing Workers and Job Competitors by Stealth

If you are poor and jobless (one of millions in the EU/Britain) and your prime minister or president says, 'Jonathan, I know you are poor and facing eviction; I know you are not employed and are searching for work, but unfortunately I am going to deliberately import one million new job competitors whom you will have to compete against as you attempt to rejoin the workforce as you search for jobs at the same time as these new one million citizens will also be searching for work,' you will be angered beyond belief. If your leader said this, he would soon lose his job and likely face an investigation to determine just how many bribes this representative and public servant accepted.

Yet when your prime minister or president says, 'Jonathan, there are millions of poor and suffering refugees who are scared and terrified, there are no other countries in the world to help them, all of the refugees must come here and remain here forever,' it is a great deal harder to feel angry in any way because it seems evil to say, 'No,' to refugees or economic migrants or to anyone who requested that you share the fruits of your labours with them, even if you have few fruits left and are facing homelessness and eviction, psychological destruction and financial destitution.

Chapter Forty-Two — What the Mayor of New York Says vs. What Potential Citizens Say

The African American mayor of New York said today (January 15th 2023) in El Paso, Texas, whilst addressing migrants/South America, that 'there is no more room in the Big Apple' for them, calling a sudden influx of migrants a 'national emergency'. He continued, stating that, 'Our cities are being undermined … and we don't deserve this, migrants don't deserve this, and people who live in the cities don't deserve this. We expect more from our national leaders to address this issue in a real way….'

New potential citizens (ignoring native concerns and warnings) say:

'There's still room left in your neighbourhood, you are not yet totally surrounded and overcrowded. Why do you need so much personal space anyway?

'And so what that you would never in a million years ever choose to live in my homeland even if I paid you millions to do so. My culture, which was born in that place and thus shaped by a place you avoid because it always seems destabilised, tense and volatile, is a valid culture according to your leaders, which means it deserves to live extremely close to you.

'So if you are a pagan Native American chief, you must tolerate the Christian churches erected 100 metres away from your totem poles and the other vestiges of that almost destroyed culture, the story of your family.

'If you speak English, like the majority, you must tolerate me speaking my native language for the entire duration of my stay, making it seem as though I am more "on holiday" than an integrated and patriotic resident.

'I am sorry for wearing the garb from my homeland in your homeland. I know you don't want me to wear this garb here, like I don't want you to wear your garb in my homeland, but this garb comforts me, it reminds me of my identity and what I chose to leave behind. But you can't complain about my garb because your leaders and teachers tell you to tolerate these things, just as Native Americans were expected to tolerate Anglo-Saxon Christians. Tolerance is a great thing; what could go wrong?

'Because your leaders tolerate us, you have to tolerate us and respect us, which means no borders and no border walls. You have no power; we have the power….'

The reason why multiculturalism exists and why mass immigration continues is all about power rather than an inspirational, beautiful and unifying culture or philosophy because if you don't voluntarily integrate, what are you doing? You are resisting the majority will. The majority will always prefer conformity and integration rather than separatism.

If you want to live with silverback gorillas in the jungle you will instantly replicate them 100%, why? Because they have less self-control in comparison to humans. If the human migrant integrates, the silverbacks will be calm and without anxiety because they instinctively see humans as a threat. We are the most dangerous species because we have problem-solving and curious minds, which guarantees our supremacy upon the occasion of a conscious infusion of human will and vigour.

Chapter Forty-Three — ISIS

The former deputy foreign minister of Bulgaria, Milen Keremedchiev, who is intimately familiar with this topic, said today, the 30th of March 2023, that, 'ISIS fighters pass through Bulgaria like illegal immigrants.'

He continued, 'Among the illegal immigrants who pass through Bulgaria, there are also those who are connected to the Islamic state. They are coming from Afghanistan—the increased migrant flow, which also passes through our country, poses a risk to the national security of Europe.'

Mr Keremedchiev was commenting on the case of the seven men recently detained in Belgium for terror-related offences and for participating in a terrorist group.

He added, 'The route of weapons (illegally smuggled guns and explosives) also coincides with that of migrant trafficking.'

After the recent arrests in Antwerp of the seven 'terror suspects' it has been suggested by multiple sources that members of what has been called a terrorist group or cell were also involved in the trafficking of illegal immigrants from Afghanistan and Syria to Turkey and then to Belgium—investigations continue.

We all witnessed the zealousness of those who fought against US and NATO-backed forces in Iraq and Syria. This zealousness and passion dies hard, and more and more it seems that it is attempting to resurface and regroup in the heart of Europe, so perhaps this is a good time to place Europe's soldiers on the border to ensure that no more guns or terrorists are able to enter. Those representatives who continue calling for open borders or a liberal approach to mass immigration and rehousing refugees will directly be responsible for each and every terror attack committed by those given refuge by the EU. Multiple convicted terrorists in the UK and Europe were once asylum seekers/"refugees".

Weakness will get you killed, whereas strength will ensure your survival.

Chapter Forty-Four — Stop Being So Naïve

Are there not conmen in England, Canada, Finland, Ukraine, Russia, and Sweden? Yes.

Are only white Europeans conmen? No, it would be racist and incorrect to claim this was the case. Crime, corruption, conmen and deception are a universal problem with most in the West knowledgeable, for instance, about the online and telephone scams that emanate from nations such as Nigeria and India.

When a good man, a Christian European for instance, witnesses huddled masses on the other side of his border, he wants to end their suffering, he feels responsible for them because he is hardworking and self-motivating and strong and capable. He pities them so phones his representatives and insists that the borders be opened in order to make him feel better in tandem with 'raising up' the innocent and good and pure individuals on the other side of the border fence, who, for some strange reason, cannot prove their national origins due to few having passports, documents or proof that they are who and what they say they are.

Those who will choose to opt in to paying more tax in order to assist non-citizens, all non-citizens without question, are not scammers or conmen. They are misguided and thinking only of the short term, but these individuals could not be called greedy or criminal or deceivers of any kind due to their insistence on helping others rather than enriching themselves. This is why they are unwittingly being deceived by many, many conmen and conwomen from abroad.

Scenario:

The EU becomes a poor union; it is overpopulated, crime is rife, sectarianism rises, life is tough. It comes to mimic certain Middle Eastern and African states from where the majority of migrants who wish to enter Europe originate.

Due to not being in the EU, Turkey remains unscathed by the changes that affect the EU states; in contrast, it becomes a paradise in comparison to the disordered and chaotic EU.

Civil wars and tribal conflicts erupt in one or more EU nations. The most vulnerable EU citizens flee to the Turkish border in order to escape the conflicts, but what happens next? The same thing that is happening today in Turkey:

Every European conman and criminal who (of course) does not wish to fight for his nation by defeating the dictator (because criminals and scammers and conmen are, by definition, anti-patriots) and every idle European who has avoided work and responsibilities his entire life joins the back of the queue of genuine refugees storming towards the Turkish border—and they begin pelting Turkish border guards with stones and rocks as others hold their babies over smoky fires in order to get them to cry for the Turkish news cameras as is happening today on the Turkish/Greek border, in reverse.

If Turkey were dense and suicidal, she would open her borders to any and all Europeans because that would guarantee that she would not be importing patriots, she would not be importing defenders; rather, she would only be importing those who are afraid to fight, can't fight or who are criminals and conmen and anti-patriots, and before too long, the European conmen living in Turkey, the European criminals and bullies and bottom-feeders would soon turn the Turkish public against genuine refugees and the genuinely persecuted, causing widespread racism and xenophobia, creating the climate necessary for a massive sectarian future conflict in Turkey—all because she was trying to help but too naïve to guess that criminals and conmen would hide themselves within the migrant waves.…

Search online the term, 'Migrant camp rape,' or 'migrant rape Turkey,' what you will learn immediately, from a wide range of independent sources, is that it is near impossible to move from Africa or the Middle East to the EU border (if you are a woman or child) without being raped or robbed. The same is true of those migrating from South to North America, with mothers often giving their young daughters contraceptive pills in advance, in anticipation of them being raped multiple times by the criminal migrants among their number.

The sad irony is the very thing genuine refugees are fleeing from travels with them in the groups moving northwards and they are latterly resettled (after being abused in a number of ways during their perilous journey) in the same refugee camps and then migrant quarters in European capital cities with the very men who raped and abused them, blackmailed them and forced them to pay "protection money" previously.

The good migrants fear the bad migrants, but the pro-open borders advocate in the West only sees migrants because he believes that only his own people are both good and bad, wrongly believing that 'all foreigners are good'. How naïve, how incorrect, how self-harming.

Do not believe me; do your own research. Just spend five minutes reading reports from charities and NGOs about the mass rape of girls and women in Turkey by their fellow migrants, the criminal migrants the EU needs to keep out at all costs.

Within minutes of beginning your research, you will discover articles from the *New York Times* with headlines such as, 'You have to pay with your body: The hidden nightmare of sexual violence on the border,' and

'Violence against smuggled migrants is widespread' from UN News (news.un.org) or 'Female refugees face physical assault, exploitation and sexual harassment' an article featured on Amnesty International's website (amnesty.org), which states, 'Women and girl refugees face violence, assault, exploitation and sexual harassment at every stage of their journey ... all women reported (to Amnesty International who were interviewed) that they felt threatened and "unsafe" during the journey. Many reported that in almost all of the countries they passed through they experienced physical abuse and financial exploitation, being groped or pressured to have sex by smugglers, security staff or other refugees.' Amnesty International is reporting that refugees are bullying, tormenting, threatening and raping other refugees during the march to Europe. What this means is on the one hand Europe is inducting terribly traumatised victims of these atrocities and on the other hand is inducting all of the perpetrators of these atrocities also, a double negative effect on Europe.

Genuine refugees, those who are terrified, those who are being actively persecuted, visit the embassy or consulate in Turkey (or elsewhere) of the nation they wish to protect them. So why are there millions, literally millions of individuals living in Turkey who all identify as being refugees who refuse to visit any embassy or consulate? This is why:

1/ Turkey is a NATO member and a safe country. If you are a refugee, you cannot pick and choose what nation you live in, it doesn't work like that. Existing rules and norms (from the UN) state that 'the first safe nation' is the nation you should remain in if you wish to be known as a refugee. If you continue migrating afterwards, you are not a refugee because the first safe country (in this case Turkey) has already given you refuge.

2/ Most of the millions of migrants in Turkey know that if their applications for asylum are rejected in Turkey, if they apply to the German or Austrian Embassy there, for instance, they will have wasted their time and money getting as far as Turkey from their homelands and they were raped and robbed and extorted on their journey in search of a 'better life' for nothing. The genuine refugee doesn't fear being called an economic migrant because he/she is willing to work, yet fake refugees (the criminals and conmen I mentioned earlier) who are driven to enter Europe due to a desire to get welfare, free accommodation and healthcare for life, something that is impossible for most natives to achieve in their homelands, is continually insistent that he is a refugee. He shouts the word 'refugee' again and again whilst hurling rocks on the Turkish side of the EU border, taking advantage of the power of that word, co-opting it as he acts in no way whatsoever like a refugee or a scared, persecuted or vulnerable individual. But asylum is a huge loophole and every conman in the world knows this fact—why would France give a man asylum and then be happy for him to become homeless the month after? There would be outrage. The refugee is a protected class in Europe, for some reason he is entitled to more than native citizens are.

I was born in England, where many people, perhaps a million or more, have signs in their windows saying, 'No canvassers, no hawkers, no cold callers.' These signs have been deemed necessary by many in England and other nations also in order to deter native conmen and criminals and bullies.

Europe needs to hang a similar sign on her southern borders because if those in the West find it necessary to warn their neighbours and countrymen not to even think about attempting to scam, pressure or con them, does it not stand to reason and make sense to assume that those who are raping and robbing and extorting and scamming and tormenting their fellow migrants on the march to Europe need to be similarly warned in advance? At the present time, the absence of a sign, warning or deterrent gives the green light to every psychopathic rapist and conman who is desperate to enter Europe in order to pleasure himself that Europeans are not willing or able to protect themselves. Such men think of Europeans as lambs to the slaughter.

Hang up the sign, Europe, if you wish to survive. Don't forget what genuine refugees are fleeing from—the fake refugees who are being resettled every day all across Europe.

Chapter Forty-Five — Interview Questions

(For Poly-interviews/as Part of Immigrant or Refugee Induction)

These are questions every sane citizen in every nation would like to ask prospective new citizens before granting them entry, protection and a share of the fruits of their hard labour:

Have you ever killed a person?
- Yes.
- No.

***

Would you still wish to live in the EU if you won €100,000,000 on the lottery today?
- Yes.
- No.

***

Have you ever raped a person, an adult or a child?
- Yes.
- No.

***

Do you know people living in the European Union who have committed crimes?
- Yes.
- No.

***

Do you plan on committing crimes in the EU?
- Yes.
- No.

***

Do you believe men and women are equal?
- Yes.
- No.

***

Have you ever been arrested?
- Yes.
- No.

***

Have you ever been convicted of a crime?
- Yes.
- No.

***

Are you a terrorist?
- Yes.
- No.

***

Do you believe that armed struggle is the correct way to achieve your objectives?
- Yes.
- No.

***

Do you have friends or family members in the EU who you know to be criminals?
- Yes.
- No.

***

Would you prefer to be rehomed in a neighbouring property of high-ranking EU officials and politicians who are pro-immigration or rehomed in a neighbouring property of politicians or members of the indigenous working class who are anti-immigration?

- I want to become a neighbour of pro-immigration politicians and bureaucrats.
- I want to become a neighbour of anti-immigration politicians and workers.

***

Have you ever tried to enter the EU illegally?

- Yes.
- No.

***

Would you like all European citizens to have a vote or referendum on immigration and accepting refugees/asylum seekers?

- Yes.
- No.

***

Do you believe homosexuality should be punished with the death penalty?

- I want homosexuals to be executed.
- I don't want homosexuals to be executed.
- Homosexuals should be punished in another way.

***

Do you believe women should be able to vote?

- Yes, women should have a vote.
- No, women should not have a vote.
- No one should have a vote.

***

Do you like democracy?

- Yes, I love and support democracy.
- No, I hate democracy.

***

Are you prepared to become a non-EU citizen if the EU nation you are settled in chooses (like the United Kingdom) to end their membership of the European Union?

That nation would become more independent and nationalist. Would you be happy being a former EU citizen in a free and independent country or do you not wish to have national citizenship and loyalties and would you continue leaving each EU nation that chose to exit the EU?

- I never want to leave the EU, so I will relocate to another EU nation if my new homeland chooses to leave the European Union.
- I am happy to lose my EU citizenship and become a German, Italian, Romanian or Hungarian if the country that provides for me and protects me chooses to leave the European Union.

***

Will you defend Europe if it is ever invaded or attacked?

- No, I won't defend Europeans because I need to be defended; I am not a defender or protector.
- Yes, I will defend Europe, Europeans and the EU against all threats.

***

Do you want to work in the EU?

- Yes.
- No.

***

Do you believe that only indigenous Europeans should defend Europe?

- Yes.
- No, all EU citizens have a responsibility and duty to defend Europe.

***

Will you remain living in the EU forever?

- Yes.
- No.
- Yes, but only if the EU doesn't change.

***

Under what circumstances will you no longer wish to gain entry to the European Union?

(You can select more than one answer)

- If the EU ends welfare.
- If native jobs are offered to native people first and if the minimum wage is increased enough to encourage poor natives to want to work.
- If there is no more free healthcare.
- If there is no more free housing.
- If there is no more liberalism and tolerance.
- I want to live in the EU/under the EU regardless of circumstances, nothing can change my mind.

***

Should everyone in your new EU nation, including protectionists, nationalists and libertarians, be forced to pay higher taxes to pay for your accommodation, healthcare, education and welfare, etc.?

- Yes.
- No.

***

If millions of foreigners were granted residency or asylum in your homeland, would this increase or decrease native racism and xenophobia?

- It would increase racism and xenophobia.
- It would decrease racism and xenophobia.

***

If the EU grants you asylum, will you consent to being resettled in an EU country of our choosing?

- Yes.
- No.

***

If the EU grants you asylum, will you consent to being entered into the Resettlement Lottery?

- Yes.
- No.

Chapter Forty-Six — Stand and Fight

What would the effect have been on the English and British people if outside saviours had come to their rescue before they managed the lofty feat of overthrowing tyranny and beheading King Charles the First? If outside saviours had swooped in and offered asylum to the British people that monarch would have remained on the throne and democracy, as it currently exists in the UK, would look very different indeed.

What would the effect have been if outside saviours had come to the rescue of the people of Scotland when Emperor Hadrian's legions approached, seeking to conquer them? Hadrian's Wall wouldn't exist today because Rome would have seized the entirety of the British Isles.

What would the effect have been if outside saviours had offered to feed and water and house every disaffected and downtrodden Frenchman on the eve of the storming of the Bastille? France wouldn't have democracy today, nor would it be a republic. I am sure many French desired some sort of miraculous rescue, yet because such a thing was absent they chose instead to risk death by storming the Bastille, destroying fascism, destroying autocracy, destroying the dictatorship, smashing elitism.

But imagine if aliens or Russians or the EU or whomever had miraculously appeared and stopped them and said, 'No, no, please don't storm the Bastille; please don't behead your king; please don't stand up to fascism. You don't need to spend so much time, energy, money, blood, sweat and tears because we are pro-refugees, we love refugees. You don't need to fight; you don't need to be strong; you don't need to be independent; you don't need to be the very best your species, your tribe has ever produced. No, your ancestors were strong and fought, which is why you're here. But you don't have to fight, you shouldn't fight because we're benevolent and loving, so come to our countries, you can even retain your philosophy, religion and ideology instead of adopting ours. You don't even have to speak our language; you just have to stop fighting.'

The man who says he loves refugees doesn't love refugees, he merely wants to tame them—he wants to tame humans. He couldn't imagine storming the Bastille; he couldn't imagine holding back legions of Romans, causing Hadrian to build a great wall across Northern England because Hadrian, like the European Union, like the United States of America, hated unruly people and the people north of Hadrian's Wall were unruly. They cared about something far more important than wine and wealth and power and watching men and animals be slaughtered in the coliseums for the pleasure of psychopaths and nihilists; they cared about independence, they were the ancient Brexiteers.

If the European Union (and their pro-immigrant/pro-refugee stance) had existed in 1789, the year the Bastille was stormed and liberated, France wouldn't be France today. It would be something very different because when there are nations and systems that not only condone running away from your problems and running away from your duty but actually encourage this, it creates national apathy, national depression and national surrender.

If all the French had to do was climb over a wall or climb over an EU border fence to receive a free apartment for life, free healthcare for life, free food for life, free pensions, free protection, free education and free legal services and translation services, how many would have stood and fought against tyranny? How many millions would have been tempted by the lure of all of these free things?

If you love humanity, tell every man who runs from a fight, tell every man who abandons his post, tell every man who rejects his duty, tell every man who abuses the rare privilege he has of being alive, the privilege he has of being able to fight, the privilege he has of being a human being, of being wise, of having the propensity to be great, tell him, 'Stop and turn around.' Otherwise, the one man who works the hardest will soon find himself supporting and feeding every other man on the planet (the EU is the one man).

Is this man God? Is this man kind and loving or is this man a fool?

The other men who come to be kept and protected by the one man who is hardworking and responsible will very soon become irresponsible (because the one man does everything for them) and will all produce many children who will also come to the one man in search of his large charitable teat, in search of an easy life, and in so doing will cause the corruption of mankind. Their lives will become pointless, their purpose will be lost, and their purpose being no longer present will cause these men to slowly destroy themselves.

Ashamed of themselves and their actions, these men, these users, these dependants shall surely destroy themselves due to the shame and confusion they feel because every instinct in them urges them to build a house with their own two hands, to wrap that house around themselves and around their precious families, which they would die for, which they would kill for, which they would do anything for regardless of the danger—what man runs from danger? We *are* the danger.

Stand and fight, stand and fight, stand and fight.

Stand and fight against tyranny; stand and fight against evil; stand and fight against bullies; stand and fight against gangs; stand and fight against apathy; stand and fight against depression; stand and fight against fatigue; stand and fight through the pain and grief; stand and fight against anxiety and fear.

You are men. Do your duty. You are human, which means you are a living marvel. You can achieve anything; you can move mountains. And never believe that dying in pursuit of a noble cause is failure because it is success: You automatically lose every fight you avoid but automatically win every fight you embrace when your motivation is pure and true.

What good is existence if you spend it in another man's house?

What good is existence if you spend it nomadically avoiding every conflict? We are built for conflict. Do you not have two fists? Use them!

Stand and fight; save yourself and your family by demanding independence, responsibility, work, toil, struggle and self-governance.

Live your life joyously, fully, with nothing held back and humanity shall eternally salute you, rather than eternally pitying you and keeping you.

Stand and fight and you will win or abandon your home and you will lose—we will all lose.

Chapter Forty-Seven — The REAL Face of the UK Left

(This chapter originally appeared in the book *The Sudden and Unexpected Multiculturalisation of Mayfair, Kensington and Belgravia — Which Ended Mass Immigration and White Flight in the UK*)

In truth I am far more the 'face of the left' than the current order that exists in the British Isles, who are now Left+*. They still share leftist and socialist principles, yet have come to artificially create and then hold true to (for political reasons/short-term advantage only) multiculturalism and mass immigration and ever more also the creed of open borders, internationalism, one world and of rejoining the EU—which would be the end of UK democracy.

(*Left+ = the pre-existing ethno-socialism (national socialism, in effect) + progressive neoliberal wokeism and tolerance, which translates to reactionism and surrender and weakness and an absence of leadership or direction—adaptation to unwanted, unpopular and undemocratic changes created by authoritarianism and brute force and big business and greed rather than a self-chosen course of action based upon philosophy or ideology or belief in multiculturalism being superior to monoculturalism, for instance).

Scenario:

All non-natives suddenly vanish, they are all transported (think the transporter tech from *Star Trek*) to another planet far away, a paradise with all of their possessions and houses and religious buildings and every facet of the cultures that were imported post 1960 into the UK (sixty years' worth of changes reversed in a single second).

What is left are the indigenous communities, the Anglo Saxons and Celts and other ancient indigenous tribes, as well as the UK right and the UK left and centrists and those on the various fringes.

Question:

Would the UK Conservative Party or the Liberal Democrat Party or the Labour Party still be 'pro-mass immigration and pro-multiculturalism' the day after?

Would these main parties (the current largest parties) cry and cry and moan and squawk until Britain became, once again, undemocratically transformed against the will of the native working class into New York City?

Would the left in the UK and the union movement continue talking about racial equality and would the left in general desire to immediately replace the non-natives who had vanished with new non-natives from 10,000 miles away because of, for instance, a deep hatred for homogeny and the indigenous folk?

If Britain were homogenous in 2023 in the way it was in 1950, and Britons witnessed the race riots in Paris and the BLM riots and marches in the USA and culture clashes occurring everywhere outside the borders of the UK, would a single Briton accept or tolerate a single non-native entering the UK? No. Because only a select few privileged or damaged individuals are masochists, entire races cannot be masochistic; the tribes of Britain are not masochists, which is why they did not vote in favour of mass immigration or multiculturalism or white flight.

The cynical attitude from the left and the establishment is 'Some have come, so we better just accept it and keep our heads down.' What apathy and cynicism and weakness and absence of leadership.

Yet, it goes far beyond and deeper than this.

Now the left have become cheerleaders for mass immigration and resettling refugees and self-abnegating by increasing taxes for the indigenous poor in order to benefit the non-indigenous at home and abroad. They are in direct competition with the Conservative right, such as Boris Johnson who once said, 'I love Europe, we are European … I love immigration, I am a pro-immigration prime minister,' and has long desired Turkey to join the EU, both before and after Brexit.

Cameron spoke in the past about desiring to have an Asian or black prime minister in the future, which would be shocking if he were Asian saying he desired a white prime minister of an Asian nation, shocking and down-talking the qualities and abilities of the indigenous people.

There is no difference between the mainstream left and right in UK politics as both are desperately keen for votes, they both follow trends and their eyes are ever fixed on opinion polls rather than on indigenous suffering and the white flight they woefully ignore to their eternal shame—if black flight were occurring in an African nation in 2023 due to unlimited immigration from Europe, the world would declare the leaders of that nation to be complicit in an act of state-sanctioned demoexpulsion of natives. The world, the UN, everybody would call the leaders of that nation 'anti-indigenous' and anti-black racists—especially if the black leaders of that African nation were endlessly saying foolish comments such as, 'I can't wait until white men and white women become prime ministers and presidents and rule over us.'

The UK left does not want immigrants, only big business wants immigrants.

The UK left does not love multiculturalism because it requires ever more police and CCTV and surveillance inside mosques and other imported places of worship and community centres and houses and business premises and endless trials into FGM and honour killings and one thousand other un-British practices, which deplete our resources, time and patience and sanity.

Bring back the death penalty in tandem with privatising the failing NHS and the immediate result will be five million or more guest workers (what non-conformist and non-integrating self-segregating communities could be described as) will leave within one calendar month and no more migrants shall ever arrive in dinghies or in the back of a truck or within the undercarriage of an aircraft ever again—because migrants and refugees are attracted to liberalism and weakness and generosity and stupidity.

They do not come to be near to the taxpayers who will house and feed and protect and keep them despite them refusing to become British and continuing to wave the flags of other nations; no, they only come because they know the neoliberal hedonistic and guilt-ridden elites and big business and special interests control Britain rather than the working class because the working class have been undermined and their power supressed by destructive waves of mass immigration, which has fragmented and balkanised the UK, which threatens her very existence.

Of course now all realise that Enoch Powell was right, just as Churchill was when he gave the same warning about the dangers of multiculturalism a few short years earlier, covered elsewhere within this work. Unlike the recent arrivals since circa 1960, whose act of self-segregation evidences their knowingness of the unpopularity of mass immigration and multiculturalism in the UK, the native Brits would not flee abroad if the NHS became privatised and if the death penalty returned and if all men were stirred to once again 'dig for victory', as in that moment of monumental change, the Briton shall once again be in his natural element and will embrace struggle and privation and labour as it feels right in his heart to do so. He will be shocked when he sees millions of self-segregators voluntarily flee abroad, and only then will he know the truth of his own spirit and theirs also.

In that moment the natives will realise that such folk were only ever fair-weather citizens as most abandoned their ancestral homelands for one reason only—money. Ask the Indian-born doctor who left India after she raised him and taught him everything who needs his help more, his kinfolk in India or white Anglo Saxons thousands of miles away in rainy England? It is only about money, be the immigrant impoverished or well educated, and all leave voids in their homelands, voids and demotivation. The same ethnic Indian doctor in the UK is proud of the fact that he can say for a certainty that ethnic Indians own India, despite his presence and the presence of other economic migrants who are similarly fair-weather citizens causing indigenous ethnic Englishman to no longer be able to say ethnic Englishmen own England.

Privatise the NHS, disallow welfare and benefits for all naturalised citizens and non-citizens, bring back the death penalty and no more economic migrants shall come. We must break the cycle, we must snuff out the flame that attracts the cause of our decline if we desire to remain sovereign as currently we are on course to lose several cities and then counties in the coming decades, with a situation similar to what occurred in Serbia/Kosovo absolutely guaranteed to be replicated before too long due to the terrible mismanagement of our once respected kingdom.

We must also let the Commonwealth go her own way; those nations that demanded independence automatically became our competitors, some would say enemies, when they sought to 'go it alone', we should respect their wishes and offer no further support or association. We must chart our own course as we lurch towards complete self-sufficiency and independence in keeping with the will of the majority of the British people—white flight was and is a vote against the entire current liberal political order and against immigration and against multiculturalism, this is undeniable.

Brexit was a vote against globalisation and mass immigration, this is undeniable. The British people desire independence, majority native rule and monoculturalism. The British people want their country back, just as Gandhi wanted his country back, just as Martin Luther King wanted respect rather than vilification and hatred—what the millions of refugees fleeing from multiculturalism in the UK will tell you they feel; vilified, unloved, degraded, demonised and silenced.

If the transporter tech existed and if all arrivals post 1960 were able to be peacefully transported to a planet far away where they could start a new civilisation together, just separate non-British migrant communities who will likely continue self-segregating and choosing monoculturalism on an individual basis (which is natural and healthy), it would be impossible, actually impossible for big business and the left or big business and the right to recreate multiculturalism in the United Kingdom as after the indigenous peoples had a taste of it, of the hundred or more languages, the culture clashes, the white flight, the race riots, the imported gang culture and crime, imported terrorism and the need for the bobby to suddenly be armed to the teeth, they would never again allow their nation to become changed and balkanised and broken just so the NHS can exist or just so the few at the top can buy a second yacht or fourth mansion.

Would the 95% of Britons who voted no to recreating the "paradise" that existed the week earlier, before all non-natives were transported far away by throwing open the borders once again to one and all from the four corners of the world, be called horrible evil knuckle-dragging little Englander fascistic racists? No, no they wouldn't, because they would no longer be prejudiced as they had experienced the unwanted and pro-big business undemocratic changes in their ancestral homeland, they had plenty of time to judge politicians and the migrants who refused to integrate as they so hated Britain and so hated the British people. Rather, the 5% who voted in favour of restoring multiculturalism and mass immigration would be the only ones who could possibly be called "haters" because they would know by their actions that if they got their way once again, the vast majority, millions and millions of Britons, would be made absolutely miserable and depressed and detached and suicidal as a result.

If I hated India, I would try to import millions of Pakistanis and Welshmen and Somalis and Libyans and Texans into India because that would really hurt Indian men and women, especially the poorest, those on the bottom rung of the lowest ladder, as suddenly they would feel far more inferior and worthless than they felt just the day earlier as now there would be new people above them, new races and cultures and religions above them that they must respect and tolerate or be given ten years in prison for "racism" and "thought crimes".

If I hated any nation I would desire to create multiculturalism in that nation as that would be the quickest route to nihilistically destroying that nation as, sooner or later, culture clashes would occur, then balkanisation and then the creation of Kosovos and Donbases—and when these things occur in the West, just know the cause: Big business, greed and liberal tolerance. I refer you to the twenty types of pro-mass-immigration advocates chapter at this stage, it provides a greater overall picture of the people and groups who will be the cause of titanic destruction if further empowered and listened to.

Chapter Forty-Eight — Immigration, Gender and How to Rapidly End Multiculturalism

(This chapter originally appeared in the book *The Sudden and Unexpected Multiculturalisation of Mayfair, Kensington and Belgravia — Which Ended Mass Immigration and White Flight in the UK*)

In relation to native men having little problem with non-native women moving to and then fully integrating into their community, this example of an interaction in a multicultural nation may go some way to explaining why xenophobia is on the rise in places such as the UK:

An entire community, multiple extended families, moves lock stock and barrel in a herd fashion, even exporting their imam from Islamabad to the UK where they instantly recreate their homeland in the host nation they chose to collectively move to. The newly arrived migrants are given passports and citizenship within three years. After this time many begin having children; many of the children are girls, who are raised in the same way they would have been raised if they had been born in Pakistan, with them learning languages unique to that part of the world and being raised to be Muslim also despite being born in Christian majority England.

Those girls become women and marry other second-generation Muslims due to an extremely intense effort being made by the minority community that emigrated in a collective fashion to continue to maintain its original homogenous and separate identity for a number of reasons.

The girls born in England, who were raised as though they were born in Pakistan, marry men who were born in England but raised as though they were born in Pakistan and then have children of their own, more girls, who are raised to be Muslim as they would have been in Pakistan, with the clear intent being to maintain in a nationalistic or tribasic fashion Islamic and Pakistani homogeny eternally in the host nation.

The native men know not to seek a date with first-generation migrants from Muslim communities.

The native men know not to seek a date with second-generation migrants from Muslim communities.

Thus, native men feel as though the recent additions to their country, the females who have just entered their realm, their historic and indigenous domain, are eternally 'off limits' to them and thus they deem them immediately to be eternally 'foreign' and non-integrating. If the incomer refuses to even consider marrying/dating/procreating with native men, how can the incoming migrant possibly hope to be accepted or tolerated?

This is beyond a snub, beyond disrespect; this is interpreted by most as insistence upon segregation and a vote of no confidence in native men and a disgust for native culture, creating the obvious instant impression that the natives and their culture and 'not good enough', which begs the question: 'So what are you doing here? Why did you come to my country if you don't want to join with my family and clan?'

The first-generation female Pakistani Muslim has a girl (the father is almost certainly a Pakistani-British Muslim man). The girl then becomes a second-generation female Pakistani-British Muslim. She has a girl (the father is almost certainly a Pakistani-British Muslim man). The girl then becomes a third-generation female Pakistani-British Muslim.

By now, the latest generation has seemingly integrated into general British culture, being fluent in the language and knowledgeable about the cultural norms of the natives; yet, even after two, three, even ten generations there exists an extreme problem, which prevents full integration and thus harmony and the prevention of xenophobia and hatred:

An indigenous Englishman (there is no history of migration for generations in his family, as far as he is aware his family have been present for 10,000 years in the UK, or longer, most Brits are related to all of the original tribes that have long inhabited the British Isles) is walking through his country, England, in the year 2150. He sees an attractive woman who just so happens to be a descendant of the Muslim migrants mentioned above; the woman he takes an interest in is (by that time) a tenth-generation Pakistani-British Muslim migrant.

The native Englishman approaches her in the same fashion he would approach an Anglo Saxon woman whom he desired to court, or date; yet before he can say a word to the woman, who sounds as English as himself, who lives in England and pays taxes in England and whose family have now been present in the UK for almost 170 years, a group of tenth-generation Pakistani-British Muslim males approach him and prevent him from speaking to the woman he was interested in meeting and getting to know as he saw past her skin colour, he saw past the fact that she was wearing a hijab and saw past the fact that she was unlike him in almost every way as he was not a racist, not a bigot, not prejudiced and not full of hate in any way whatsoever.

He approached the woman because he knew her family had lived in England for multiple generations and because he saw non-natives represented in the entertainment industry and business and politics etc. He assumed that now, finally, the one-time self-segregating migrants had 'become English' had 'become British' and thus the women born to the descendants of migrants who came a century or two centuries earlier were

'British women' rather than the possession of a foreign power, rather than being eternally separate.

The men demand that the indigenous Brit back off, stopping him in his tracks as they tell him, 'Stay away from our women.'

Because there will be an eternal "claim" upon females in migrant communities in the UK (as a consequence of tolerance for those who refuse to integrate, who hate the natives and who hate the native culture and way of life) it is the non-integrating and balkanising incomer who is responsible for creating the climate of xenophobia and fear, rather than the native man who would warmly welcome a date with an Afro-Caribbean woman or a Pakistani Muslim woman or an Indian Hindu woman or a Chinese Taoist woman or a ... you get the picture.

The fact that native British men are forbidden to even talk to certain British women proves that the women in question are British in law only and not in practice.

Imagine this in reverse:

In 2023, an entire working-class white Christian English community moves lock, stock and barrel to Islamabad taking with them their priest and their church and their fashion and their customs and culture, which they fully expect the natives in Islamabad to not only accept but to tolerate and love, which causes instant Pakistani flight in Pakistan and culture clashes. Then imagine even 150 years or more later when the local native Pakistani Muslim men are not permitted to even speak to the white English Christian females in the self-segregating migrant communities who moved to Islamabad not because they loved the culture or the people but for reasons of personal advancement and due to their homeland becoming overpopulated.

Would a Pakistani Muslim man in Islamabad whose ancestors had lived in that land for a thousand years or more be happy about this situation? Would he ever consider the non-integrating white British Pakistanis whose loud church bells compete with the call to prayer in Islamabad to 'be Pakistani' if he was unable to date/marry tenth-generation women from that separate community? Would he consider any individual present within his nation who refused to intermarry with the native Pakistani Muslims to be a Pakistani? Would he not think it rude and intolerant? Would he not request that the migrant community repatriated itself to a nation more suited to their needs? Would he not consider the refusal to bear his children to be a huge snub for the native Pakistani people and proof of deep and profound racism and xenophobia, and wouldn't this then cause him to become xenophobically minded?

If the Pakistani native man in Islamabad only observed white English Christian women relocating to Islamabad who immediately integrated, did not form ghettos or enclaves and who warmly welcomed converting to

Islam and Pakistani cultural norms and fashions and all else in between, would any Pakistani native man in Islamabad feel xenophobic or maligned or inferior or full of anger or feel as though he needed to choose either 'fight or flight'? No, of course not, as in that scenario there would be no problem, no problem whatsoever, just as if only non-native women moved to the UK multiculturalism would not exist in 2023. There would be only one culture, British. Monoculturalism would also have been possible if the men who guard "their women", even if the women are second- or fifth-generation British citizens, were tolerant and respectful rather than tribal and separatist.

To say, 'She is too good for you,' which is what is implied when arranged marriages continue in migrant communities in the UK as well as very un-British things such as FGM and honour killings, is revealing as to the true opinion of self-segregating herd communities about native Englishmen and native Britons, as the community is happy to benefit from British protection and order and public services and the NHS and certain cultural aspects they like, yet they find it an abhorrent thought to consider "one of theirs" marrying into a white Christian family or an Afro-Caribbean Christian family, for instance.

The division and xenophobia all of this causes is immense, with all walking on egg shells afraid of causing offence, afraid of asking the "wrong woman" on a date, fearful that she will be killed by her own family/tribe for speaking to a native (despite her being a second-generation migrant and desiring adoption of the culture) or fearful that he (the native man who defeated fascism, who defeated Hitler) will be physically attacked by the migrant community he invited in because he is tolerant and loving and progressive and masochistic and short-sighted and thought it would have been fascistic of him to demand that migrants leave their old ways in the old homeland or remain there. When in Rome you must do as the Romans unless you wish to replace the Roman or cause them to come to regret inviting you in.

Multiculturalism can work but only if all incoming migrants are tolerant, only if all migrant men are instantly happy on day one for their sisters and aunties and daughters to date and marry native men who do not look like them, who have a different religion and language and way of life.

If this is impossible, if migrant self-segregating communities cannot bring themselves to integrate and be tolerant and respectful of the natives and their culture and ways, they need to find a land where all are like them—their homeland, the place they left voluntarily.

Gender plays such a huge and monumental role in the immigration debate. This is not a black and white issue but an issue of masculinity and machismo and male pride and ego and tribalism.

For instance: Native women hear about refugees struggling in their homeland, they see photos of lots of young and healthy-looking migrant men in dinghies crossing the Mediterranean in the hopes of starting a new life in the West. They empathise with them; they chant, 'Open the borders.' Why? Because they are females and the incomers are males.

However, if these same women, who claim to only be motivated by reasons of love and unfettered compassion for humanity (despite there being mass native poverty and homelessness, which they wilfully ignore), observed that in the migrant boats there were only super-attractive super-model-type female migrants, each one looking more exotic and mesmerizingly beautiful than the next, all with hypnotic eyes and incredibly toned figures and perfect hair and incredible posture and confidence and vitality and allure, would they be half as vocal about 'letting them all in'? Hell no, one thousand times no. If the migrants are only female, beautiful and exotic it will anger the native women of any land; whereas if the migrants are only males is will anger the native men of any land.

Women in Britain are happy to tolerate self-segregating migrant Muslim communities as the women in those communities are no threat to them; they are kept in their communities and will invariably marry Pakistani-British Muslim men or Somali-British Muslim men or Sudanese-British Muslim men or Turkish-British Muslim men. The second that Muslim communities in the UK become uber tolerant and progressive and engage in a 'reformation' by relaxing their views on intermarriage and integration with the host people who have invited them in and who protect and aid them in every discernable way an interesting thing will occur. Native men will become less xenophobic as native women become more xenophobic due to the hundreds of thousands of new female competitors they have to contend with. Many native women will overnight ban their boyfriends or husbands from leaving the house without them; they will be keeping an eye on their man at all times.

Their husbands will not be permitted to volunteer their time down at the community centre that helps disadvantaged and poor refugees if said refugees are all females in their late teens or early twenties. Think about it. 'Hi, my name is David. I just saved you, I rescued you from your horrid plight abroad by allowing you to beach yourselves on my shores, and now I am feeding you and providing you with shelter. Do you want to go out on a date sometime? Want to have a meal with me, maybe a few drinks?'

There is no way native women would tolerate this. Ergo, refugees are only tolerated for so long as there are very young and very old in their number and many men also—who will keep the female refugees far away from the native Western saviour men....

Issues such as these, facts such as these, make uncomfortable reading, yet it is essential for us to be honest and open when tackling these issues as to remain silent would be to damn us all to a predictable inglorious and dour future, which would look something like South African apartheid or US segregation. I want neither thing to occur in my ancestral land, my homeland, Britain, where every woman should be a potential wife for me or my son, rather than only being limited to a certain pool of citizens who receive no more rights or freedoms or respect than the separatist communities who wish to remain separate spiritually, religiously and genetically.

We should all be able to agree that moving to the homeland of a man and then banning that man from marrying your daughter is terrible, with most considering this elitist, supremacist, racist and anti-native, even dehumanising. After white Europeans moved to South Africa and racially and culturally kept themselves apart, creating apartheid, much of the world condemned the white South African separatists. So why do we tolerate this situation in reverse in the West? Why do we adopt a double standard here? These are rhetorical questions, we all know the answers: profit, profit, profit and liberal guilt in tandem with Marxist education and idealism and intellectual minnows with Daddy issues playing about with social engineering.

End multiculturalism now, wherever it exists. All incomers need to become native immediately, as it is in the USA, as it is in all sane nations. If you don't want to integrate, if you think the native men too low or too impure to become husbands for your sisters and daughters, why are you living in that place? Why don't you move once again? Why is your "forever home" a place you hate full of people you hate?

The native white poor, who have traditionally been scapegoated by the architects of failed multiculturalism, who have been labelled bigots and little Englanders and white trash and all manner of classist and incorrect terms, would be happy and content in this hour with no thoughts of voting far right were it not for whole imported migrant communities who dislike them so much that they refuse to intermarry or integrate.

The native does not need education; he does not need to be told to be more tolerant. The native man in Islamabad does not need to be told he should tolerate Pakistani flight in Pakistan; he does not need to tolerate the intolerable situation of an ever-increasing number of women who are Pakistan citizens, just like he is, who receive the protection and all the welfare and rights and rewards granted by being a Pakistani citizen who are 'off limits' to him, who are racially or culturally or religiously so superior to him that he is forbidden to even talk with females from the self-segregating migrant communities, let alone intermarry with a member of this separate and protected class.

The migrant always has a choice:

Remain He can the same in the land of other men who were good enough to allow him safe harbour and citizenship and protection, who were gracious enough to share the fruits of their labours with him, which will cause culture clashes, xenophobia, mistrust, hatred and division and sectarianism or change, despite changing causing harm to the ego and to pride, it seeming as though one is committing treason or abandoning their people or god/s.

If the homeland or home religion is so important to you, please stay in your own country.

If, however, he truly loves my country and my culture, he can make the choice immediately to change, to integrate and to allow Britishness to wash over him. To remake him in our image.

Be absorbed and become us or please leave, so say all of us.

The second-generation Pakistani Muslim in England who is erecting a mosque in an area where white flight occurred a few years prior due to his arrival, where no indigenous Britons now remain, thinks he loves the fact that mosques are being built in the UK. Yet the same man would viscerally hate for a single new church to be built anywhere in Pakistan or in Saudi Arabia. He calls himself British when it suits him, despite the double standards and inflicting upon the native British people acts that would drive him towards protest and even violence and worse if it happened in reverse. Just because you can continue wearing the garb of the homeland because the natives are seemingly tolerant does not mean you have to continue wearing the garb of the homeland because natives will begin asking, 'Why are you here if you don't want to be like us? And if you don't want to be like us and if you don't want to marry into our families then can you please leave immediately, because by not integrating you cause us all to be demoralised and depressed and engage in white flight and to feel lesser and soon to be under your yoke.'

Migrant tolerance and integration, rather than native tolerance, is the solution. Natives should not change one iota in any land to adapt to those invited in by big business only. No vote has been held on immigration or multiculturalism—why? Because 99% of people in 1950 in the UK would have voted 'No,' just as 99% of Pakistanis would vote 'No' today if given a vote on immigration into Pakistan.

Either non-natives need to force themselves to become nativised, achieved via conformity, integration, immersion into the culture, full adoption of the language and more tolerance and humility as they ask the natives what they expect of the newcomers or they need to choose voluntary repatriation. Two choices; two very different solutions to the problem of failed and toxic neoliberal and incredibly short-sighted multiculturalism.

Our separate cultures are represented by borders, national borders. We already had multiculturalism with each nation keeping the religions and races and cultures apart. If we are to continue to have multiculturalism and immigration we might as well dispense with all national borders and nation states also, which is one of the reasons those on the fringes of the left are so fully supportive of mass immigration, believing that long-term they can use the lack of homogeny as a means to 'unite the workers of the world'. Yet, as is now observable, long before that dream, that fantasy, could ever occur (which would necessitate a global one-world dictatorship to keep order, which no man should desire) the self-segregating and unhappy migrant communities would have become so separate and so tribal and protectionist that rather than social engineering creating world harmony, it would instead cause the creation of hundreds of new micro nations across European nations and elsewhere as a result of balkanisation caused by mass immigration and multiculturalism, a result of weakness and a lack of resolve and strength and character and hutzpah and love for the national culture and heritage and race and religion.

The solution to the multiculturalism dilemma is:

Integrate and be tolerant and love the natives and become native.

Or leave.

Chapter Forty-Nine — Final Thoughts

Whatever your political position or ideology, whatever your point of view, it is inarguable that that there exists inequality between Eastern and Western EU nations, with the former being used in 2023 as a scapegoat and whipping boy for the Western EU (liberal) states who refuse to accept any blame for being the magnet that causes hundreds of millions of non-EU citizens to fantasise daily about 'becoming Europeans' by simply climbing over a fence and running towards Berlin, Rome or Paris. (EU citizens save money for many years for their retirement, whereas millions of non-EU citizens in Africa and Asia save money for many years (including right now, as I type these words) to pay people smugglers in the coming months, years and decades to install them in the wealthiest Western European EU nations.)

Whatever your position or belief system, one and all can agree there exists a problem because if we were to open the gates on the EU's southern border, every city and town in Europe would collapse under the weight of an almost limitless flow of humanity emanating from Africa and Asia. This would not aid these people, nor would it aid any class of people already present within the EU, including first and second-generation already settled migrants.

Yes, there is a problem, and, yes, this problem needs solutions, but are the solutions mentioned herein really what are needed?

Do we really need fleets of airships and blimps painted in proud EU livery?

Do we really need 1,000 polygraph machines on the border?

Do we need migrant spies to continually disrupt the activities of foreign criminal networks?

Do we need to police who can and cannot buy food and diesel in Europe?

The long list of suggestions mentioned herein seems absurd because this situation is absurd and anxiety-inducing. These measures may soon be implemented, however, despite the fact that I bring them to your attention for no other reason than to highlight EU failures on the border and to remind EU bureaucrats that the European people require order, stability and their ancient cultures, traditions and values to be honoured and respected, rather than eroded, marginalised or ignored—native flight must end immediately.

If I were an EU citizen today I would fear the future because I would have absolutely no idea what my town, city or country would look like in five years or in fifty due to the "gift of EU freedom of movement, tolerance and charity" attracting every separatist, minority and tribe on planet Earth to the wealthiest EU nations—which would demotivate me just as it demotivates EU citizens because the millions who have already made the journey and the millions more who will make the journey in the coming years only come due to the work ethic and self-motivation of Western European men and women. If Europeans all suddenly became lazy and apathetic, illegal immigration would cease to exist within the hour.

If you don't fix the leak in your roof, it will get worse and soon your house will flood. The leak needs to be fixed immediately, within minutes of you noticing it. Why are you ignoring the leak? (I speak to EU voters and EU politicians.)

This is a rhetorical question. I know the reasons, I know you are afraid of being labelled a racist (a fate worse than death apparently), but is the pope racist for living behind twenty-foot-high impenetrable stone walls? No.

I know also that it is easier to allow millions of illegal immigrants into your lands, where they can eke out an existence within the grey economy, becoming your prostitutes, cleaners, cooks, gardeners, builders, road workers, restaurant workers and, of course (famously), pickpockets and organised beggars and smugglers of every variety and terrorists, which is why many look the other way due to the middle and elite classes' hunger for imported drugs, cheap labour and sex-trafficked and terrified young women. Shame on these selfish, self-serving people, they are the ruination of the civilisation their self-sacrificing and heroic ancestors fought so hard to create.

It is easier to do nothing, to allow this belligerency to continue, to acquiesce to the collective will of non-EU citizens who are devoid of the tolerance, sensitivities and softness and kindness (and thus weakness/vulnerability) of the modern European who dutifully salutes every passing gay pride march whilst booing every passing war veteran march and applauds like the mad bird who smiles when the cuckoo usurps his nest when his church is converted into a mosque whilst spitting and cursing at the man who politely asks for a referendum on EU membership, whom he calls an evil, deplorable fascist monster, worse than Hitler.

If the EU continues to fail the nation states of Europe in terms of mass immigration, unwelcome demographic change, minority rule, anti-democracy and native-flight, we all know what happens next. You don't need to be psychic or a prophet to predict the inevitable outcome: Grexit. Bulgexit. Deutschexit. Frexit. Romexit. Hungexit. Polexit. Italexit. Spanexit. Portugexit. Belgexit....

All it would take to prevent this would be the immediate implementation of Opt-in taxation; yet, the EU will likely instead choose the opposite course of action—banning and burning this book, which I will consider to be the act that signifies the beginning of the end of the EU experiment and a return to independent nation states throughout Europe and the abolition of the EU and latterly NATO.

Without Europeans, Europe will cease to exist because Europe is not a place; it is a collection of peoples.

Conclusion

What the EU is doing to control illegal immigration is not working, which is why this book exists. If there was not a problem, there wouldn't be a 70,000-word book in front of you in this moment.

What I find hilarious is that whenever a seemingly radical proposal is floated (a progressive proposal), such as asking potential EU citizens common-sense questions before entry, the defenders of the EU shout loudly that, 'We must remain true to EU principles and obligations and philosophy.' This means not changing, without realising or accepting the truth that the situation in Europe is only worsening in terms of overpopulation, sudden and shocking demographic shift, native flight and culture clashes. Everywhere the far right are making gains; everywhere nationalism is on the rise. I wonder why....

The instinct of these defenders of the EU is to attack everything and anything not in agreement with them, yet this is self-harming to them as, clearly, the status quo isn't working as there exists great discord between EU nations and between EU indigenous citizens and illegal immigrants, economic migrants and refugees. The EU is far too confident in its ability to keep the native worker down at heel; this overconfidence will cause its collapse unless EU 'lines in the sand' are not hurriedly drawn all around the periphery of Europe.

If a suddenly overpopulated and overstrained Europe (due largely to mass immigration—refugees, economic migrants and illegal immigrants) stops functioning due to there being more people not working than working, the collapse of the institutions that twenty million recent arrivals (legal and illegal) rely on for their continued survival and happiness will return the latest EU citizens and citizens-to-be to their pre-EU condition—being on their own again.

Those who demand entry into the EU do so solely due to the existence of EU institutions and government departments.

It is a demand, there are millions of non-EU citizens who will never turn their backs to the EU and look elsewhere to relocate. Whether you like it or not, you MUST fix this growing problem and fast if you desire a good quality of life for your tribe, community and family. But if you hate yourself and are a pessimistic-masochist, of course you will not try to fix this problem because you are one of its architects.

Those amassed on the EU's southern border do not want to be "enriched" by living near to white Christian people who drink alcohol and eat pork, no, no, no, no. They will seek to live as separately from indigenous Christian Europeans as possible, self-ghettoising and being the cause of white flight concurrently, ensuring segregation, rifts, tensions and unending anger, xenophobia, double standards and disquiet.

About the Author

Bruce Masters is a British author, psychologist, and optimist, a campaigner for democracy and peace, and a campaigner against globalisation and political and religious extremism.

A prolific author, Masters has written over 50 books spanning multiple genres: political, psychological, self-help and sociological as well as fiction, hoping to improve, educate and inspire.

In addition to being known for his revolutionary Peace Book series (including *Six Ways to Prevent WWIII* and *How We Will Create Peace in Ukraine and the World*) and his Capitalism and Democracy series of books Masters is a leading researcher and writer in the fields of autism, neurodivergence and atypicality. His suite of books relating to these subjects includes *Autistic Jesus, The Führer of Asperg: A New Understanding of Fascism, Autism and the Third Reich, ConjectureMania, The Christ Conspiracy, Tripartheid* and *The Continuation of the Origin of the Species*.

Bruce is a man of many talents and interests: a political observer and analyst, researcher and occasional satirist.

When not writing, he leads a quiet life with his family and is thankful for having the drive, knowledge and will required to birth so many unexpected, empathy-multiplying and thought-provoking political, psychological, and sociological works.

Bruce's books are very much like Marmite: You will either love or hate his unapologetically bombastic and forthright 'tough love' writing style and his leadership-heavy political and social critique and musings.

Yet one thing is for certain; you will not be bored as entertainment in addition to a roller coaster of education intermingled with opinion is guaranteed from beginning to end.

Books by the Author

(Published and coming soon)

The Capitalism and Democracy Book Series:
Book One The Political Lottery — Democracy's Last Best Hope of Survival
Book Two Capitalism Hates You
Book Three The Liberal Loophole Jails: A Peaceful and Righteous Revolution
Book Four The Cancellation of Coronation Street, EastEnders and the National Lottery
Book Five Why Charles Dickens No Longer Loves the White Working Class
Book Six Why The British Stopped Breeding
Book Seven How Nigel Farage Became Prime Minister
Book Eight The Soul Exchange
Book Nine Smartphones are Dumb
Book Ten The M25 Solution — The Creation of the Republic of London

The Peace Series:
Book One How We Will Create Peace in Ukraine and the World
Book Two Five Ways to Create Peace in the Middle East
Book Three Make America United Again: The Trump-Harris Co-Presidency 2024 – 2028
Book Four Plan C: Mutually Assured Survival
Book Five The Far Right and Far Left Are Far from Opposites
Book Six 10 EASY WAYS Russia Could Destroy Germany and the EU in 2025
Book Seven Six Ways to Prevent WWIII

The 33 Essential Questions Series:
Book One The Truth at Last! 33 Essential Questions for Conspiracy Theorists
Book Two The Truth at Last! 33 Essential Questions for Elon Musk
Book Three The Truth at Last! 33 Essential Questions for Prince Harry
Book Four The Truth at Last! 33 Essential Questions for Prince Andrew
Book Five The Truth at Last! 33 Essential Questions for Tommy Robinson
Book Six The Truth at Last! 33 Essential Questions for the Alt-right and Alt-left
Book Seven The Truth at Last! 33 Essential Questions for Christians

The UnWoke, Anti-Hate, Anti-Guilt Series of Books:
Book One Wokeism Is Crumbs from the Table of Globalist Elites
Book Two Wokeing Kills
Book Three Voluntary Taxation and Capital Punishment: For a Just, Equal and Corruption-Free Society
Book Four Escaping the Cult of Guilt: The Dark Side of Charity and NGOs
Book Five Defeating Fentanyl
Book Six Ending the Migrant Crisis in Europe: Preventing Class Wars, Race Wars and the Destruction of the EU
Book Seven The Sudden and Unexpected Multiculturalisation of Mayfair, Kensington and Belgravia — Which Ended Mass Immigration and White Flight in the UK
Book Eight Globalisation, Mass Immigration, Wokeism and Multiculturalism on Trial (Compilation of Books 1–7)

Psychology/Neurodivergence/Autism:
The Continuation of the Origin of the Species
Autistic Jesus
Don't Judge a Book by Its Cover: 21 Remarkable Similarities Between Donald Trump and Tommy Robinson
The List — The Death of Antisocial Behaviour and Noise Pollution and the Evolution of the Real Estate Industry
The Führer of Asperg: A New Understanding of Fascism, Autism and the Third Reich
Tripartheid
ConjectureMania
The Christ Conspiracy, aka The Rise of the Light Triads
The Truth at Last! 33 Essential Questions for Conspiracy Theorists

Biographical Exposés:
Russell Brand: False Prophet
One Election Please... How J.K. Rowling Bought British Politics, Hid Her True Self and Hoodwinked the World — an Unauthorised Biographical Exposé
The Truth at Last! 33 Essential Questions for Elon Musk
The Truth at Last! 33 Essential Questions for Prince Andrew
The Truth at Last! 33 Essential Questions for Prince Harry
The Truth at Last! 33 Essential Questions for Tommy Robinson

The Rowling Trilogy:
Book One J.K. Rowling In: It's a Kind of Magic

Book Two How Not to Get Sued by J.K. Rowling
Book Three One Election Please… How J.K. Rowling Bought British Politics, Hid Her True Self and Hoodwinked the World — an Unauthorised Biographical Exposé

Bruce Masters' One-Day Book Series:
Plan C: Mutually Assured Survival
The Liberal Loophole Jails: A Peaceful and Righteous Revolution
The American Altruist Assassin
Why The British Stopped Breeding
The List: The Death of Antisocial Behaviour and Noise Pollution — and the Evolution of the Real Estate Industry
Capitalism Hates You
Why Charles Dickens No Longer Loves the White Working Class
The Rule of Ten — How Prince Andrew Came to Be Exiled to Switzerland
The Political Lottery — Democracy's Last Best Hope of Survival

Fiction:
Plan C: Mutually Assured Survival
The Liberal Loophole Jails: A Peaceful and Righteous Revolution
The American Altruist Assassin
The Day Bill Gates Ended Crime
Wokeing Kills
The Sudden and Unexpected Multiculturalisation of Mayfair, Kensington and Belgravia — Which Ended Mass Immigration and White Flight in the UK
J.K. Rowling In: It's a Kind of Magic
The Cancellation of Coronation Street, EastEnders and the National Lottery
The Lord of Purgatory
Adrian Mackintosh: Agent of Karma
The Man in the Panama Hat
The Rule of Ten — How Prince Andrew Came to Be Exiled to Switzerland
The Soul Exchange
David Lammy on the Run — A Political Comedy Adventure
The Fall and Rise of a Comedy Legend!
Running Clear — How David Defeated Depression
David Lammy Still on the Run
Tripartheid
Unseeable
Zelenskyy
Vladimir Putin: Predestination
The Lord of Purgatory

The Political Lottery — Democracy's Last Best Hope of Survival

Non-Fiction:
How We Will Create Peace in Ukraine and the World
69 Excuses to Drink Alcohol and 1 Reason Not To
The Continuation of the Origin of the Species
Six Ways to Prevent WWIII
Smartphones Are Dumb
Why The British Stopped Breeding
Autistic Jesus
Don't Judge a Book by Its Cover: 21 Remarkable Similarities Between Donald Trump and Tommy Robinson
The List: The Death of Antisocial Behaviour and Noise Pollution — and the Evolution of the Real Estate Industry
Capitalism Hates You
The Internet vs. the Nationalnet
The Far Right and Far Left Are Far from Opposites
10 EASY WAYS Russia Could Destroy Germany and the EU in 2025
The Folly of Colonising the Stars: The Final Nail in the Coffin of AI and Space Colonisation
The Origin of African American Gangsters, Gangs and Ghettos
Five Ways to Create Peace in the Middle East
Make America United Again: The Trump-Harris Co-Presidency 2024 – 2028
How Nigel Farage Became Prime Minister
The Truth at Last! 33 Essential Questions for Conspiracy Theorists
The Truth at Last! 33 Essential Questions for Elon Musk
The Truth at Last! 33 Essential Questions for Prince Harry
The Truth at Last! 33 Essential Questions for Prince Andrew
The Truth at Last! 33 Essential Questions for Tommy Robinson
The Truth at Last! 33 Essential Questions for the Alt-right and Alt-left
The Truth at Last! 33 Essential Questions for Christians
Wokeism Is Crumbs from the Table of Globalist Elites
Why Charles Dickens No Longer Loves the White Working Class
Voluntary Taxation and Capital Punishment: For a Just, Equal and Corruption-Free Society
Escaping the Cult of Guilt: The Dark Side of Charity and NGOs
Defeating Fentanyl
Ending the Migrant Crisis in Europe: Preventing Class Wars, Race Wars and the Destruction of the EU
Globalisation, Mass Immigration, Wokeism and Multiculturalism on Trial
How Not to Get Sued by J.K. Rowling
One Election Please… How J.K. Rowling Bought British Politics, Hid Her

True Self and Hoodwinked the World—an Unauthorised Biographical Exposé
ConjectureMania
The Führer of Asperg: A New Understanding of Fascism, Autism and the Third Reich
Russell Brand: False Prophet
Noise Pollution Kills
The Christ Conspiracy, aka The Rise of the Light Triads
What Is Patriotism?
The M25 Solution — The Creation of the Republic of London
How to Quit Gambling This Week
You Have the Power

www.ingramcontent.com/pod-product-compliance
Lightning Source LLC
Chambersburg PA
CBHW070928260726

48661CB00003B/877